PRAISE FOR
WORK–LIFE SYMBIOSIS

"This is a powerful book. It presents a clearly thought-out and insightful model on a challenging topic. It will enable and inspire people to be at their best both inside and outside work. Everyone should read this for their own sake – embrace Work–Life Symbiosis.*"*

Tracey Rogers, Managing Director
Unilever Food Solutions UK and Ireland

"A very honest and enjoyable read chock-full of useful and practical tips to help anyone who is working in the 21st century"

Leon Neville, Director of Insights at Universal Music UK
and father of two children aged two years and four years

"Having managed many mums and dads with many different working patterns/career ambitions, I can see this book is stuffed full of practical tools for both self-reflection and taking action all grounded in real life experience"

Ann Donoghue, Experienced International HR Exec

THE MODEL FOR
HAPPINESS AND BALANCE

WORK–LIFE SYMBIOSIS

Published by
LID Publishing Ltd
One Mercer Street, Covent Garden,
London, Wc2H 9JQ

31 West 34th Street, Suite 7004,
New York, NY 10001, US

info@lidpublishing.com
www.lidpublishing.com

A member of:

BPR
Business Publishers Roundtable

www.businesspublishersroundtable.com

Printed in Great Britain by TJ International
ISBN: 978-1-910649-01-5

Cover and page design: Laura Hawkins

THE MODEL FOR
HAPPINESS AND BALANCE

WORK–LIFE SYMBIOSIS

CLAIRE FOX

LONDON   MONTERREY
MADRID   SHANGHAI
MEXICO CITY BOGOTA
NEW YORK   BUENOS AIRES
BARCELONA   SAN FRANCISCO

To Debs, Danny and Lucas
for making me happy every day

and to my parents and my brother
for always being totally amazing.

CONTENTS

WITHDRAWN

ACKNOWLEDGEMENTS

Writing this book has been an absolute pleasure, and that is largely due to the incredible amount of support and encouragement I have received from those around me. I am very grateful to my parents, Linda and Tim Fox, my brother Daniel Fox and my partner Debora Corfield. They have not only shown complete confidence in me right from the start, but have invested time in supporting me throughout this journey. Their input and ideas made such a big difference to me, and the book.

I would like to thank my two boys Daniel and Lucas Fox-Corfield for being simply incredible, fun, amazing little guys. They are an inspiration to me. I am grateful to them for teaching me to live in the moment, and for allowing me to discover enormous reserves of energy I never knew I had.

In fact, other people choosing to invest time in me and giving me opportunities is how this book came about in the first place. I will be eternally grateful to Tracey Rogers, Simone Roche and Emily Perry, without whom this book would never have been written. The following chain of events is how it came about:

Tracey Rogers introduced me to Simone Roche. Simone Roche gave me the opportunity to create and share the concept of Work–Life Symbiosis by inviting me to speak at her Women 1st conference in 2014. That led to my meeting Emily Perry. Emily Perry saw the potential for a book in my idea and introduced me to David Woods at LID publishing.

From there, the team at LID publishing, particularly David Woods, Niki Mullin and Laura Hawkins, have been excellently professional and supportive as well as a great deal of fun.

I have been fortunate enough to have had many inspirational line managers over the years. I would particularly like to thank Tracey Rogers, Nick Kitchen, Glenda Goscomb and Alan Walters (who sadly passed away last year). All of these people shaped my thinking, encouraged me and allowed me not only to grow and develop but to thrive through their exceptional capabilities, openness and personal leadership.

My friends are a constant source of support and fun and I am grateful to all of them for that. I value our friendships deeply. I would particularly like to thank Zara Hooley, whose support from the moment I even shared the idea of writing a book has been overwhelmingly positive, and Kim Craig who has encouraged me, and made me laugh throughout writing this book. I am also particularly grateful to Becky Johnson and Helen Forster who, over the years, have helped me to see things from different perspectives, and embrace a wider approach to life.

I would like to thank the vast number of people I have worked with who have inspired me, and have inspired many of the anecdotes and examples I have used to illustrate important points and concepts in this book. They have all helped me to create and share the concept of Work–Life Symbiosis.

Finally, I would like to thank all the staff at Prêt a Manger on Wimbledon Hill Road in south-west London, which is where I pretty much wrote this entire book. Their friendly and kind approach made it a pleasure to be there and an extremely productive and pleasant environment in which to work.

FOREWORD

Claire Fox's *Work–Life Symbiosis, a model for happiness and balance,* could not have come at a better time.

The world we live in is going through unprecedented change and it is widely believed that change will never again be as slow as it is today. There is also no doubt that our world, which many describe as our new normal, has become more volatile, uncertain, complex and ambiguous, all of which is making our lives more challenging as we seek to manage our professional and personal lives in a more sustainable way.

Technology has also blurred the lines between work and personal life with an 'always on' culture, significantly impacting how we work and play. The demands in our working lives can seem to be ever increasing at the expense of what really matters and many are struggling to find the balance to thrive and excel in all they do.

Claire's approach to managing this is a breath of fresh air. In a very practical and pragmatic way, backed by her own personal and humorous examples, she introduces us to a simple and powerful tool to allow the reader to take personal responsibility for finding their own Work–Life Symbiosis.

The power in Claire's approach is its simplicity and practical step-by-step method of taking control of what is really important and then building a map to manage life in a more symbiotic way. The central premise is that the relationship between work and home is fundamental and needs to be a dependent and mutually beneficial relationship. In short, one should make the other better and vice versa.

Many of us will recognise this as being common sense and a must-do but many will also recognise how difficult this is to achieve. It's easy to get caught up in the here-and-now and we can very quickly find ourselves losing perspective, thereby not finding happiness and fulfilment in either part of our lives. Claire's model provides four components with easy-to-compile checklists to deal with this. Each of the components is brought to life with examples and anecdotes, and the reader is provided with the tools to explore what it means for them personally. By the end of the book, you will have your own action plan.

In reading the book I was struck by how relevant it is for people from all walks of life – be it very senior leaders or those just starting – and how we deal with our ever increasing 'always on' world, where Work more often than not comes at the expense of Home. Claire's approach proves that both can exist and that Work and Home in a mutually dependent symbiotic relationship can provide happiness and balance.

There is something for everyone in Claire's *Work–Life Symbiosis*. I hope you enjoy the read as much as I did and find your path to happiness and balance.

DOUG BAILLIE
Chief HR Officer
Unilever
March 2015

INTRODUCTION

I once applied for a job through the internal job site of the organization for which I was working. When I got the email through confirming that my application had been accepted, I realized that I had applied for it not as Ms Claire Fox, not even Miss or Mrs Claire Fox, but as 'Sir Claire Fox'.

Awkward.

I didn't get the job, but I did subsequently work for the recruiting line manager in another role and we had a good laugh about it.

As you will have realized, I am not a 'Sir' nor am I a 'Dame', in fact; but what I am is a person with experience of making tough choices, and by and large, feeling that these choices have been the right ones. And I'm happy; happy with my life and my decisions. I have been a human resource director in large global organizations for more than eight years now, I have been working four days a week for more than two years, and I have two boys who, at the time of writing, are two and four years old. I exercise regularly and spend time with friends and family. I have never consistently worked longer hours than I am happy to work. People assume that is because I have children, but even before then, I never worked long hours because, although I am very ambitious about my career, I also love all the other things in my life that I do when I am not at work.

I have always had a high need to achieve. I think that's just my personality, but also I grew up in a family of competitive sports people. When I was younger I was a white water slalom canoeist. I competed for the Great Britain Junior team and captained that team to the Junior World Championships. I also competed for the England Senior Team, and I won a number of international competitions. When I stopped competing seriously I coached the England team for a period of time and then joined a samba band. I felt I needed to do something completely different. With the band, I performed at the Theatre Royal Haymarket in London's West End and in a performance that supported the comedian Jo Brand.

This may sound like a self-congratulatory boast, but the point I'm making is that I have always been highly ambitious about everything I do. When I left university after completing a degree in sport science and a Masters in recreation management and started work, I felt exactly the same about my career. I wanted to do as well as I possibly could. But that didn't mean I suddenly stopped wanting to put time and energy into the other things I enjoyed or stopped getting energy, excitement and satisfaction from other things in my life such as sport, friends and family. A job and a career are part of the rich tapestry of life, not the tapestry itself.

Over the years, colleagues and friends have often asked me how I manage not to work late every night, or at weekends, given that I have had a successful career to date and held senior roles in global organizations. Now that I work part-time people also ask me how I manage not to work on my non-work day. I always answered these questions, but in the past was never quite sure of the answer.

In the summer of 2014, I was asked to speak at the Women 1st conference, on exactly this subject. At first, I was terrified – I wondered what on earth I could have to say in which people would be interested, let alone from which they would benefit. I considered this a great deal, and decided that, although I may never be the world's best ever HR director (don't tell my boss please), what I do seem to do better than many others I see around me is align my life to what's most important to me and make the brave, tough choices needed to do this. I sat down and thought hard about how I do this. To my surprise, I quite easily came up with the four things I believe are critical to achieving what I call 'Work–Life

Symbiosis'. I presented this at the conference and realized that, actually, people found it extremely useful.

This made me see that I have something worth sharing and so I am sharing it in this book.

You can use this book in any way that suits you best. You may want to start at the beginning and read it cover to cover. You may prefer to dip into the sections that most jump out at you. I would advise though, whatever your approach, that you first read chapter 1, 'The concept of Work–Life Symbiosis' – as this introduces my philosophy, and chapter 2, 'Be true to yourself' – as this is the cornerstone of achieving Work–Life Symbiosis.

At the end of each chapter, you will be able to complete your own action plan and by the time you've finished the book, you will be clear on what you want to do differently, and how you are going to do it.

Claire Fox, February 2015

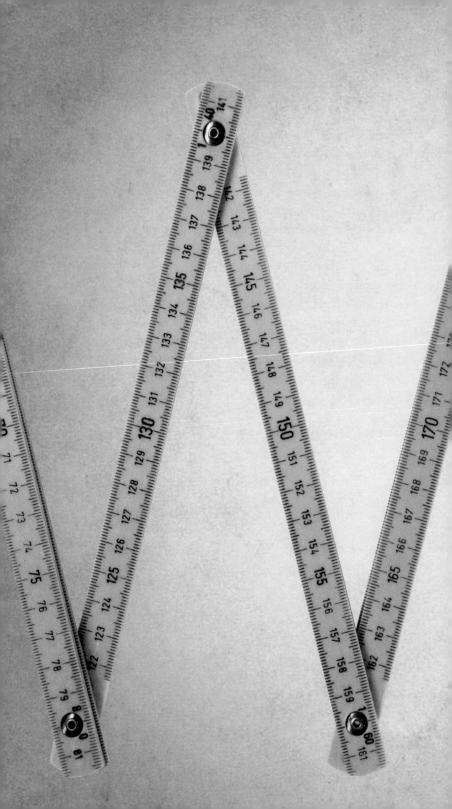

THE CONCEPT OF
WORK–LIFE SYMBIOSIS

CHAPTER

1

THE CONCEPT OF WORK–LIFE SYMBIOSIS

THE WORLD WE LIVE IN

If someone could wave a magic wand and change the way you spend your time and energy on a daily basis, would you jump at the chance?

I don't know many people who are genuinely completely satisfied with the set-up they have in terms of work, family, friends, leisure time, health, exercise, and, in particular, stress levels. The incredible shift in our use of technology in the past ten years has meant we are constantly contactable, have 24-hour access to almost any information we could want, and spend a great deal of our time multi-tasking.

I love the fact that I can check the latest news, train times or the weather on my phone wherever I am. It's amazing how easy it is to keep connected with people, sharing photos and videos while out and about on a daily basis.

This technology saves us a great deal of time; no need to spend ages planning your car journey route, just switch on the sat nav (assuming you have a signal of course); no need to work out for yourself which tube or bus line you need, just tell a journey planner where you want to get and it'll do the rest; online shopping can be done on a smartphone in the 10 minutes you have between appointments. For the most part, as long as you have signal and battery life, technology has revolutionized the way we live our lives for the better.

It has also revolutionized the expectations people have of us. We are expected to be available and responsive for a significantly larger proportion of the day than we would ever have been in the past. Employers may expect us to keep an eye on our emails in the evenings and at weekends; friends and family may want us to get back to them instantly on 'instant messenger'. The speed at which it is *possible* to get things done and organized has become the *normal* expectation.

Across businesses and industries there has been, for a number of years, a relentless focus on cutting costs, much of which is enabled by this increase in technological capabilities. For us, as employees, that means fewer resources and, unfortunately, not always less work, but still the expectation is there of constantly delivering. Contradicting this, there is increased expectation among both men and women that it is possible to have a career and spend the desired amount of time with your family.

In many ways, technology enables us to do this. In some professions and industries it is now much more commonplace to leave work in order to meet another commitment, and then to work at a later point in the day. But the ability, basically, to access whatever information we want from wherever we want, and the culture of always being available, very much blurs the line between work time and non-work time. This makes it significantly harder to control, to balance, and to ensure that we are investing the amount of time and energy we want to invest in the different areas of our lives that are important to us.

The truth is, of course, sadly no one will wave a magic wand for us to enable us to achieve this balance. We have to wave that magic wand ourselves.

THE BALL IS IN YOUR COURT

Our lives are in our own hands. It may not always feel that way, but it is the case. Mahatma Gandhi shared the powerful insight that:

Happiness is not something ready made.
It comes from your own actions.

We all make decisions every day that impact our lives. They may seem small at the time; whether to go for that run or not, whether to have a muffin with the flat white, whether the flat white should be skinny or not, whether to take the kids to the park or put the TV on for them so that we can get on with the washing. If you do get to the park, there's the choice of whether to play with the kids while they're on the swings or to check Facebook or emails. Then you have to decide whether to have salad or a pizza; to eat dinner at the table with your partner having a conversation or on the couch watching Netflix; whether to log on after dinner to deal with those last few emails; whether to call your mate who left a message earlier; whether to have that early night as intended. All these small decisions we make on a daily basis add up to a pattern and form habits that become the way we live our lives, very easily indeed.

Don't get me wrong; I'm not saying we should never sack off going for a run and sit on the couch eating pizza, watching a film. Of course we should, life's too short isn't it?

The important question, though, is what is your norm? What's your daily rhythm and routine? Are the decisions you usually make in these situations the ones you want to be making? In fact, how do we know what the decisions we want to be making are anyway? Do we know what's really important to us in life? I mean REALLY IMPORTANT? When the chips are down, what or who comes above everything else? If we aren't totally clear on this, we have nothing on which to base the decisions in our lives. We need to align our choices with what matters. If our choices are not aligned in this way, we need to ask ourselves:

WHAT IS STOPPING ME MAKING DIFFERENT CHOICES?

It may not be easy, and the reality of some of the decisions you could make may be difficult, but the fact that it is difficult is exactly why so many people in the world are not happy with their mix of work and life.

A good friend of mine is an excellent and very experienced accountant. At one point, she took a job at KPMG: the *crème de la crème* of roles one might think! What an amazing opportunity. Great money and benefits, a high kudos job in a leading, renowned professional services firm. But it wasn't her. She stayed for a year and left to work for a national charity where she was significantly happier with the culture and far more engaged with what the organization was actually doing. From the outside, many professionals would deem the KPMG job as the 'better' job, but better for whom?

And who decides what is 'best' anyway?

THERE'S NO RIGHT ANSWER

I certainly don't have all your answers. In fact – and this is of critical importance,

> THERE ARE NO ANSWERS THAT ARE 'RIGHT',
> THERE ARE ONLY ANSWERS THAT ARE 'RIGHT FOR YOU'

Sheryl Sandberg, chief operating officer at Facebook and author of famous 2013 book *Lean In: Women, Work, and the Will to Lead* talks passionately about women in the workplace and some of the reasons for the serious imbalance between the number of men and women in senior leadership roles across all organizations and careers. She suggests women who want to stay in the workplace need to 'lean in' to their careers, pushing themselves forwards, having confidence in themselves, and accepting the wider life implications of treading the path to the boardroom.

This is fantastic advice for both men and women whose priority in life is to be as successful as possible in their careers. But what about all those talented, smart, successful women and men who could make significant contributions in the boardroom but also want to have the time and space to invest in things outside work that are important to them? It is a small percentage of women, particularly in comparison to men, who ultimately want to sacrifice as much of the rest of their lives as is currently necessary to end up being on a FTSE 500 board of directors.

If Sheryl Sandberg put the same amount of time and energy into telling men to 'lean out' as she does to telling women to 'lean in', I wonder whether this would help re-balance the number of men and women in senior roles?

What I mean by this is that if we want gender equality in leadership positions – whether that's in business, politics or our community – we need to make these positions accessible and appealing to as broad a range of women as possible. If it only appeals to the small number of women who want to be fully focused on their career to the exclusion of having significant time for other things, we will never achieve gender balance. We need current boards of directors and leaders in all walks of life to embrace a sustainable relationship between their work and their lives. We need them to have Work–Life Symbiosis.

Of course, what's right for you depends entirely on what's important to you and what you want to achieve. That may involve leaning in, it may involve leaning out, it may involve not leaning at all. As I said in the introduction, I want to be highly successful in my career – but just because I have a job, it doesn't mean I no longer also want to achieve and be successful in other areas of my life too.

I passionately believe we need to follow our dreams and live by our values. Of course, we also need a dose of reality with that and to understand that we have to make choices in order to achieve this. But in doing this, we will lead happier, more fulfilled lives.

So my message to you is this:

Take **control** – it's your life. Know what's really **important**. Make **choices** and accept the consequences.

Remember that the only person who can make change is YOU. And whatever you do, don't have regrets.

WHAT IS WORK–LIFE SYMBIOSIS?

Years of research and commentary have gone into the area of work–life balance, and plenty of books have been published claiming to help you do less of one and more of the other.

It seems to me that for many people this hasn't been very effective. Why? Because this thinking has developed more into the idea of 'work–life integration': perhaps an evolution in this area because 'balance' never really worked out...

Work–life integration is the idea of blending what you do professionally and personally in order to make both work. This approach tends to be appealing and effective for some, but less so for others. For me, the expression brings to mind the professionals I see in the park with their children after school, who are on their BlackBerries. They are integrating instead of balancing – they have left work early in order to pick up their children from school. They can do this because they are able to use their smartphone to continue to keep on top of their emails and phone calls. The result, I fear, risks two things:

1)   Frustrated and disappointed children who desperately want their parents to pay attention to them and notice how cool it is that they can get to the top of the big climbing frame now

2)   Poor quality of work being done for the employer because it is basically impossible to concentrate fully on, and engage with, something with so many distractions

I see work seeping into every corner of people's personal lives as a result of technology and 'integration' – checking emails early, late, at the weekends, on holiday. I do not see personal stuff getting much of a look-in during work, other than perhaps managing to put the washing on during a 'work from home' day, phoning the insurance company or going for a quick run at lunch time, and perhaps making (the second half of) the school Christmas play.

Work is an enormous part of most people's lives, both in terms of time spent and value attached. It seems to me that striving to achieve 'balance' is underselling the value I can derive from things in my life that are so important to me. Balance implies you mustn't do too much of one because it will be to the detriment of the other. Integration doesn't work for me because it makes things blurred around the edges – when I'm playing with my kids I want to be 100% focused on them and not distracted, and when I'm delivering something for the business I want to give that all my attention too.

I think we should expect something more from these two broad categories of activity in our lives of 'home' and 'work'. I think one should positively enable and facilitate the other. The relationship between home and work is fundamental - it is such an integral part of our lives - it needs to be **symbiotic**: a dependent and **mutually beneficial** relationship.

> EACH SHOULD MAKE THE OTHER BETTER

Unfortunately, I suspect we've all seen examples of people being ground down by work. Think about a colleague or friend who gets a big promotion they've always wanted. They are so excited and really feel like they've 'made it'. Then you see them a few months later and they look like a shadow of their former vibrant self. They look tired, worn out, stressed and they've got quite a few more grey hairs. You ask them how they're getting on in the new job and the response lacks the enthusiasm it once would have had and they tell you how busy it is and how much there is to be done.

You have ask yourself, is that really what they wanted? Is it really worth it? And how is this impacting on the rest of their life?

I know a great number of people who are in, or who at some time or other have been in, a negative cycle between home and work. They have a stressful day at work, don't get all the things done that they wanted to (because the expectation was completely unrealistic anyway) and so feel that they haven't achieved what they should have. They are exhausted, and they are annoyed because they have left the office later than they intended AGAIN.

They bring all these feelings home with them and this effectively ruins their evening. They have no energy to invest in their personal relationships or activities, they have little time because they are late home and often have more work to do, their partners, children or friends are annoyed with them because they want to see the happy relaxed person they once knew again. The individual knows the negative impact this is having on their personal relationships and their health, so they resent the situation. They don't get a good night's sleep because they are stressed and anxious and they resent work more the next day because of the negative impact it's having on the rest of their life.

I make it sound too bleak perhaps, but a lot of people experience this to a greater or lesser degree at some point and I suspect it doesn't sound completely unfamiliar to you.

So this is where we need Work–Life Symbiosis. We need to short-circuit this negative relationship and turn it into something positive.

THE WORK-LIFE SYMBIOSIS CONCEPT

The long and short of it is, when we are happy and content in our lives outside work we take energy, enthusiasm and positivity into work with us. This enables us to be on top form in the work place. We radiate that energy and this impacts on those around us positively. Basically, it enables us to be more successful in our roles. We enjoy and embrace being at work rather than just getting through it or, at worst, resenting it. We then come home from work buzzing, excited and energized meaning we embrace our evening and weekend and are able to focus fully on our family, friends and activities that have given us this energy in the first place. This allows us to gain yet more energy and to refuel for the next day or week at work.

This positive, symbiotic connection between home and work, meaning we get more out of each because of the other, is often not what people experience. I know everyone has tough days and we can't always skip home full of the joys of spring, but we can always find positive things in our day, and we can all certainly make sure that we get more energy from work than we give to work.

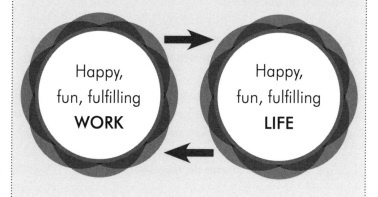

THE WORK–LIFE SYMBIOSIS MODEL

There are four key components to achieving Work–Life Symbiosis:

1) BE TRUE TO YOURSELF

This is having absolute clarity about what's really important to you in life. I mean the **big things**, the things that, if the world were ending, you would care about above everything else. Then, keeping this clarity, and aligning your life choices behind it.

2) BE (ABSOLUTELY) FABULOUS

It's easy to get stuck in a rut, especially if we are dissatisfied with our situation. But we all know that when we are at our best, we have a louder voice and greater opportunity. We need to understand how we can be our best self, all the time.

3) RUTHLESSLY PRIORITIZE

Easy to say, hard to do! Whether we work part-time, full-time, or are in one job that used to be two jobs, freelance or a job-share, we all need to be better at this and it's key to success.

4) HAVE CRYSTAL-CLEAR BOUNDARIES

Know what is and is not ok for you because this will be different from the next person; communicate it effectively and protect it – no one else will do that for you!

The four components themselves are critically important, and so is the way in which they interact with each other. They are interdependent.

This book will take you through each of these elements in detail, bringing them to life with examples and anecdotes, and will provide you with tools to help you explore what it means for you personally.

Then you will be ready to wave the magic wand yourself.

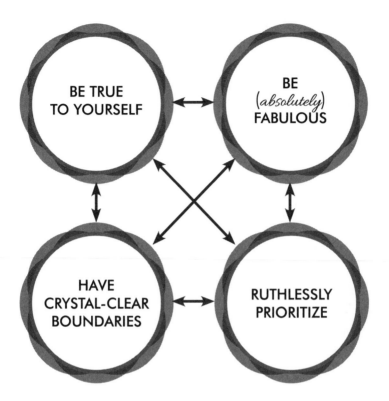

BE TRUE TO YOURSELF

CHAPTER

2

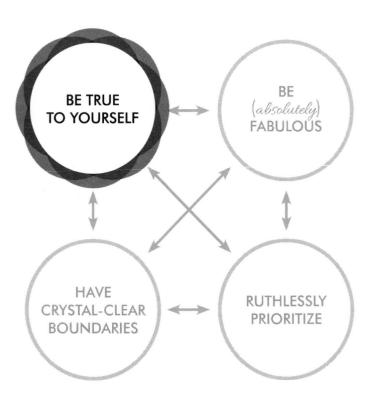

BE TRUE TO YOURSELF

WHY THE FILM *LEGALLY BLONDE* HAS A STRONG MORAL MESSAGE

You may wonder what a film has to do with working long hours but this film has everything to do with it. I've been a long-time fan of the 2001 film *Legally Blonde*, starring Reese Witherspoon. My friends all see this as a bit of a trashy rom com (sorry Reese), and laugh at me when I say it has a strong moral message. But actually Elle Woods (the lead character for those of you who haven't yet had the pleasure of watching the film) is, in the face of teasing, bullying, social rejection and cruelty, crystal-clear about what is really important to her and what she values, and she sticks to it. In the end, those around our heroine look past her frothy blonde exterior and see her for the wonderful, strong, kind, intelligent woman she is, with the highest levels of integrity, and end up being her best friends. As she is such a kind person, she forgives all prior sins and embraces their new-found appreciation of her. I suspect I may not have been so forgiving. But then, I'm not Elle Woods.

We all need to find our inner Elle Woods.

The concept of being true to yourself is the cornerstone of the Work–Life Symbiosis model. It may sound obvious, easy even, and to a degree becoming clear about what's important to you at one point in time is relatively straightforward. It's keeping it at the front of your mind and living your life by it that's the hard part.

Sadly, a colleague of mine passed away recently. He was an amazing, well-respected and loved individual, and in the days immediately after his death I had numerous conversations in the office where people said things like "It really makes you think about what's important in life" or "This certainly puts everything into perspective". And it does, it really does.

But the issue is that it's very hard to keep a grasp of that newly found perspective. Within a few days, everyone is back on the treadmill of life, sprinting as fast as possible just to stop themselves flying off the back. What's 'really important' in life becomes once again relegated to the important but not urgent box, and is not revisited in any meaningful way again until the next tragedy that makes everyone stop and think about the fact that our lives are finite and could be over in an instant.

LIVING YOUR VALUES

Most people tend to live their daily lives by their values to some degree or other. But aligning your life behind them, and behind your other life priorities, is another thing entirely. I am someone who is naturally confident, open and honest. It's in my DNA and it's how I was brought up. I'm the sort of person who will always point out to the waiting staff in a restaurant that they have missed the bottle of wine off the bill. I call these 'good for the soul' moments. You get opportunities in life every now and then to make the right choice, and doing so always feels good, even if it costs you the price of a bottle of wine.

It's not always easy to live by your values though. My partner is a woman, so being as open as I naturally want to be can be challenging in some situations. The decisions I've made through my life about this, though, very much reflect the fact that honesty and integrity are core values for me. It has always been more important to me to be honest when someone asks me if I have a boyfriend or husband than to avoid potential awkwardness, embarrassment or judgment that might come from telling them I'm gay. And, so far, this has pretty much worked out fine. My (now) wife and I were shouted at in the street once in Chester by teenagers because we were holding hands. They were a very safe distance away and shouted "lesbians" just loud enough for us to hear. I thought to myself 'yep'. I do remember being called a dyke quite a few times in the student union bar, but I was usually too drunk to take any notice.

I know some people have experienced, and still do face, terrible homophobia in their lives, and I realize I have been lucky not to have done so. I have also been extremely fortunate and privileged to have completely supportive and wonderful family and friends. I have found, particularly since having children, I get interest and intrigue more than anything else. Once people realize I'm perfectly happy talking about myself (basically, until the cows come home), they want the low-down on how I got pregnant; how we decided it would be me and not my wife; where we got the sperm; whether the father plays a role, and so on. The point is though, I came out when I was 17 and that decision was based completely on the values I hold.

When I joined a corporate multinational as a graduate trainee, I very much wanted to build relationships and fit in with everyone. But I certainly wasn't going to lie to avoid risking being the 'only gay in the village'. I remember a few weeks went by and I was in the slightly awkward position of having mentioned my 'partner' but with everyone, of course, assuming it was a man. I was anxious about it because I find when people don't know it can feel to me like a bit of a 'thing', a barrier, especially in work situations. If you tell people too quickly, you are at risk of being accused of 'shoving it down people's throats'. If you leave it too long it looks like you've been 'living a lie'!

Anyway, it was soon to be resolved. The whole team went for a drink after work one day and in a group conversation I was asked my boyfriend's name. So I grasped the opportunity with both hands and said "well it's funny you should ask that because actually…. It's Marion". You could see the recognition on people's faces as the cogs turned and they worked out that, therefore, it was a girlfriend and not a boyfriend. Except one brilliant person who hadn't made the connection at all and loudly piped up with

"No way! I used to know a bloke called Shirley!"

This was the best thing that could possibly have happened for me because all the attention (and quite honestly raucous laughter) was now focused on her and not me.

An excellent outcome to coming out.

HAVING A LIFEBOARD

To be true to yourself, you first need to get clear on what matters. For this I use "what I like to call" (reference for *Miranda* fans) a 'Lifeboard'. For the designers among you, you can think of this as a mood board of what's important in your life. Essentially, a type of collage of words and pictures representing everything that really counts for you.

To illustrate this, I have included my own Lifeboard. We all tend to have big buckets of areas that are important, for example family, friends, career, and my Lifeboard may look quite generic to you because you would expect much of what features to be there for everyone, and it may well be. The key though is making **choices**. This is not about capturing every single thing that is important in your life – this would likely be a long exhaustive list that would not help you align your life choices at all. This is about the things that are **more important** than other things.

For example, travelling and playing a role in the local community are important to me, but when I forced myself to narrow down priorities, they were less important than other things at this point in my life. You will also see that money doesn't get a look in and my job and career don't feature as strongly as they would for some people, being in the 'lifestyle and achievement' section of my Lifeboard rather than in a section of its own. For some people, excelling in their career may well be their number one or number two priority in life. I love my job, and my career is important to me, but achievements in other areas of my life are also important. My work dominates more time of course, because I need to earn a living, but in terms of my life overall, the importance of work to me is proportionately smaller than the time spent on it.

On the following page is my Lifeboard right now.

To create your own Lifeboard you need to challenge yourself. And once you have it, it won't just be a pretty picture. The point of doing it is more about what the implications of it are than the board itself. For example, what are the choices you're making in your life in each of these areas? Are there choices you are making that are driven by other factors that on reflection should not be shaping your decisions?

There are four steps that will help you shape your thoughts for your Lifeboard.

1) Make choices
2) Know your values
3) Imagine the future
4) Get in touch with your defining moments

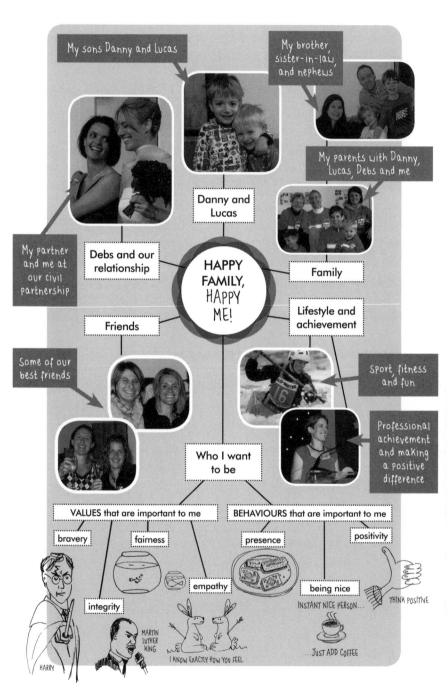

My sons Danny and Lucas

My brother, sister-in-law, and nephews

My parents with Danny, Lucas, Debs and me

Danny and Lucas

My partner and me at our civil partnership

Debs and our relationship

Family

HAPPY FAMILY, HAPPY ME!

Friends

Lifestyle and achievement

Some of our best friends

Sport, fitness and fun

Who I want to be

Professional achievement and making a positive difference

VALUES that are important to me

BEHAVIOURS that are important to me

bravery

fairness

presence

positivity

empathy

being nice

integrity

INSTANT NICE PERSON...

THINK POSITIVE

HARRY

MARTIN LUTHER KING

I KNOW EXACTLY HOW YOU FEEL.

...JUST ADD COFFEE

Civil Partnership photo - Harptrees photography
Claire's Speaking Engagement - Women 1st Shine Awards 2014

Let's look at these steps.

1) MAKE CHOICES
You have to force yourself to make choices. To start with, ask yourself:

WHAT IS THE *ONE* MOST IMPORTANT THING IN MY LIFE RIGHT NOW?
You don't need to tell anyone if you don't want to! Also keep in mind this may well change and evolve during different phases and stages of life, and that's perfectly ok. Is it your children? Your partner? Your job? Your career? Your best friend? Your sporting achievements? Your musical ability? Your volunteering? Your health? Your wealth? Keep in mind, it's not important **what** it is, there's no judgment here. I don't mind whether you say it's your bank balance or your first-born child, the important thing is you **know** what it is. Then think about the second, third and fourth most important things.

Make sure you differentiate between what is actually important to you, as opposed to what other people might think should be important to you! The idea of getting clarity on the big things is of course not new. Dr Stephen Covey, a hugely influential management guru and author of *7 Habits of Highly Effective People* (published in 1989) talks about the "big rocks in life". You can find a cheesy, yet quite insightful, video about this easily on YouTube (search for 'Stephen Covey big rocks'). He is effectively saying that you need to fill your life with the big, important things first and then add some of the small things around the edge afterwards, so long as there's room. Otherwise, your life grows full of all the small, perhaps urgent but not important, things that take up our time, energy and brain space and there's inevitably no room left for your 'big rocks' in the end. So, make sure you know what your big rocks are. Capture your thoughts on this on the following page:

THE NUMBER ONE MOST IMPORTANT THING TO ME IN MY LIFE IS

....

....

....

THE NUMBER TWO MOST IMPORTANT THING TO ME IN MY LIFE IS

....

....

....

THE NUMBER THREE MOST IMPORTANT THING TO ME IN MY LIFE IS

....

....

....

THE NUMBER FOUR MOST IMPORTANT THING TO ME IN MY LIFE IS

....

....

....

2) KNOW YOUR VALUES

Values, as defined by the 1995 edition of *The Concise Oxford Dictionary*, are "one's principles or standards; one's judgement of what is valuable or important in life". They are key drivers for most people, and form the bedrock of our personalities, in my opinion. Yet it is hard to be clear on which four or five are your absolute priority.

For example, if I ask you to read the list of just 20 example values suggested below, out of an almost endless list that could be considered, I suspect you would nod your head and agree with most of them. Probably we all would. But if I asked you to choose the one or two that resonated with you the most – the ones that really jump out at you – you might see yourself making different choices to the next person. If one person chooses achievement and another sensitivity as their most important value, they would very likely approach running a team meeting in a completely different way to each other, and so it should be with our choices in life.

Example values: honesty, determination, tolerance, reliability, positivity, justice, empathy, discipline, sensitivity, trustworthiness, achievement, calmness, accountability, autonomy, flexibility, excitement, professionalism, resourcefulness, healthiness, making a difference.

Looking at a list of values helps to give you some direction, but it's also important to consider what your life experiences tell you about your values. The *Mind Tools* website (www.mindtools.com) sets out some useful questions in its 'What Are Your Values?' section, written by Ruth Hill and the Mind Tools Team, which I think are well worth considering:

i) **When were you happiest in your life? Think about a few examples from your personal and professional life.**
a) What were you doing?
b) Were you with other people? Who?
c) What other factors contributed to your happiness?

ii) When were you most proud? Think about a few examples from your personal and professional life.

a) Why were you proud?

b) Did other people share your pride? Who?

c) What other factors contributed to your feelings of pride?

iii) When were you most fulfilled and satisfied? Think about a few examples from your personal and professional life.

a) What need or desire was fulfilled?

b) How and why did the experience give your life meaning?

c) What other factors contributed to your feelings of fulfilment?

Then ask yourself what these experiences are telling you about what's important to you in life and what you value. Try and find words that capture the essence of what you have described.

If you feel as though you need some additional input or direction, try visiting the 'Free Stuff' section of a website developed by Jane Sunley (www.janesunley.com), CEO of Purple Cubed and author of *It's never ok to kiss the interviewer* (published in 2014). She has a useful free on-line e-values tool which takes ten minutes to use and can help broaden your thinking and make priority choices between the many values areas. If you have identified words or areas from the questions above that are not there you can add them yourself to ensure the exercise is a strong reflection of the areas that are most important to you.

Now that you've given it thought, capture your top five values here. You can always refer back to the list of 20 values at the start of this section if you want a reminder of the sort of thing you might consider:

MY TOP FIVE VALUES ARE:

1 ....

2 ....

3 ....

4 ....

5 ....

3) IMAGINE THE FUTURE

It's your retirement party at work. You unfortunately had to work until you were 79 due to lack of adequate pension provision, but at least you've made it now. A colleague is making a speech about you. They are talking about what you are like as a person, what they loved about working with you (and, of course, mentioning a few light-hearted things they didn't like), what they'll miss about you and what they've learnt from you. What would you like them to be saying? How would you like to be described? With this in mind, do you make the right behavioural choices now to be on track for that description? For example, if you would value someone saying that you always had time for people when they needed your help and support, consider whether you do actually make time for people when they need help and support!

Capture your thoughts over the page:

AT MY RETIREMENT PARTY I WOULD BE PROUD, HAPPY AND HONOURED IF PEOPLE SAID THE FOLLOWING ABOUT ME:

....

....

....

....

....

....

....

ON A SCALE OF 1-10

(1 BEING 'I'D BETTER BUCK MY IDEAS UP - NO ONE IN THEIR RIGHT MIND WOULD SAY THIS ABOUT ME RIGHT NOW' AND 10 BEING 'ABSOLUTE NO BRAINER - PEOPLE WILL DEFINITELY SAY THIS ABOUT ME ALREADY'),

WHAT IS THE LIKELIHOOD OF THIS COMING TRUE BASED ON YOUR CURRENT BEHAVIOURS AND CHOICES?

1   2   3   4   5   6   7   8   9   10

I was immensely touched by the speeches at both my dad's retirement party and my mum's leaving work do. I felt incredibly proud to be their daughter on both occasions and wondered whether there was a cat-in-hell's chance of anyone saying stuff like that about me when I retired. Then I realized that, in actual fact, that was totally up to me. The pressure is on.

Back to imagining. A few months later, it's your 80th birthday (you had to work until you were 79 remember). You're in excellent health, by the way. One of your family members, perhaps a child, sibling or friend but certainly someone who's known you personally for a long time, makes a speech about you here too. Again, talking about what they love about you, how they have experienced you, what you bring to them personally and to the family, what sort of person you are. What would you like them to be saying? Challenge yourself to consider whether you are making choices now that will lead to this.

Capture your thoughts on this here:

ON MY 80TH BIRTHDAY I WOULD BE PROUD, HAPPY AND HONOURED IF PEOPLE SAID THE FOLLOWING ABOUT ME:

ON A SCALE OF 1-10

(1 BEING 'I'D BETTER BUCK MY IDEAS UP - NO ONE IN THEIR RIGHT MIND WOULD SAY THIS ABOUT ME RIGHT NOW' AND 10 BEING 'ABSOLUTE NO BRAINER - PEOPLE WILL DEFINITELY SAY THIS ABOUT ME ALREADY'),

WHAT IS THE LIKELIHOOD OF THIS COMING TRUE BASED ON YOUR CURRENT BEHAVIOURS AND CHOICES?

1   2   3   4   5   6   7   8   9   10

The funeral of the colleague I mentioned was brutally honest. This is what he had wanted. There were many wonderful, heart-warming, kind things said about him. There were also a number of references to the amount of time he spent at work and the fact that this took him away from his family. He achieved an incredible amount in his career and was extremely successful, contributing not only to the organizations he worked for but, greatly, to the people he worked with, including myself. It made me wonder whether, on reflection, he regretted those choices and whether, in the end, he wished he had spent more time with his family. Or perhaps he accepted that the path he chose was the right one and the resulting value he gained and added through his professional career was equally important and worthwhile. I deeply hope he didn't have regrets.

4) GET IN TOUCH WITH YOUR DEFINING MOMENTS

I think people have defining moments in life that they remember. Things that happen that crystallize an idea or concept for them. For example, I remember being in the car with my mum, as a teenager. It was during the time when I was seriously into my slalom canoeing, and I was focused on it to the exclusion of a great deal else. I was moaning about the fact that mum had said I couldn't have a new 'cag' (a cagoule is a waterproof top and in this case one that is specifically designed for canoeing) to replace the current, perfectly sufficient, but not completely cutting-edge, one that I already had. She had said that because of the recession we couldn't afford it. Having not really grasped the gravity of a recession-hit economy I said "If it wasn't for this bloody recession, I could have a new cag" to which my mum immediately replied "If it wasn't for this bloody recession there would be a lot more people with a roof over their head". That shut me up, I can tell you.

I will never forget that conversation and I will never forget the reality check it gave me. Thank you, mum.

I can remember the exact moment when I first decided that 'being present' was something that was very important to me, and something at which I wanted to be better. I was in a European job at the time at a big multinational as an HR director. I was in a four-hour meeting. There's the first issue perhaps. Should any meeting really last four hours?! Anyway, there were some biscuits in the middle of the table. I saw them and thought how nice they looked. I had one. Some others had one too. Not everyone. It was lovely and I was hungry. I wanted another one, but I'd only just had one – was that rude? How long should I leave it before having another biscuit? How many biscuits were there, compared to the number of attendees? How many of the attendees hadn't had a biscuit yet? Was that because they didn't want one at all, or just that they didn't want one yet? Would I look greedy if I took another biscuit? If I got a coffee perhaps it would be ok, as it's pretty usual to have a biscuit with a coffee, right? I had another biscuit. It was really good. So, I'd had two and some people had had none. Would there be any more biscuits if these ones were finished? I really should leave a longer gap before having a third. Would anyone else have three biscuits or would that just be me?

It went on like this the entire meeting. I was totally distracted. This meeting was about selling a €6 billion part of our business with 3,000 employees and all I could focus on was the biscuits (just to be clear, I was the junior HR person in the room). Now, I'm sure we've all been distracted in meetings by thinking about shopping, the weekend, the kids, whatever (haven't we, or is it just me?), but this was too extreme for me! I decided that evening that I would never ever let that happen again. I decided that, if I was going to attend a meeting, I would be completely present and add value, and if I thought that I couldn't do that, I would not attend. I'm certainly more effective in meetings as a result of this little incident.

The importance of presence has been reaffirmed more recently for me too – having children has made me live in the moment more than I ever did before. I remember going to pick up my son from nursery one day when he was just over two years old. He had learned a new song that day that I'd never heard him sing called *Wind the Bobbin up*. When I arrived, he sung it over and over again to me with such gusto and enthusiasm, actions and everything. It was so incredibly cute (it really was, I'm not just saying that as his mummy, even you would have thought so…). I paid attention, but I also remember thinking "I can't wait to get home so that he can sing this to my partner too because she'll love it". Of course, he never ever again sung that song in that way, with that much enthusiasm and excitement, not even when we got home ten minutes later. It was a once-in-a-lifetime performance, that I had the pleasure of witnessing. Having children has certainly reinforced for me that there are plenty of things in life that can't be recreated so you'd better focus completely on them when they are happening, because really in life, every moment is a once-in-a-lifetime moment.

Reflect on what the defining moments have been for you, and consider what they tell you about the person you want to be. Have you behaved differently as a result of any of them? What has changed?

Capture your thoughts on this here:

THE MOMENTS IN MY LIFE THAT HAVE HELPED TO DEFINE ME ARE:

CREATING YOUR LIFEBOARD

Now that you have taken these four steps, you are ready to create your own Lifeboard. Everyone's will be different. You may find it reveals something you didn't realize consciously, or that it makes you reconsider timings. Your priorities might surprise you; your choices may force you to admit something you hadn't previously admitted, or you may find they reconfirm what you already thought. Whatever happens, you will have it and it's there to remind you. I worked with someone on this recently, and when she showed me her Lifeboard, she had put it all on the backdrop of a heart, which was perfect because it demonstrated her passion for the many important things in her life. Some people have more words, some more pictures – either photos or drawn or cut from magazines, it doesn't matter, it's what works for you.

This is quite an open and free exercise, there is no specific format you need to follow because it's just about creating your visual representation of the things in life that are most important to you – your life priorities. They may be linked to one another or they may be completely separate, standalone things. They can be people, relationships, places, values, activities, objects, even feelings. There are only three guidelines for this exercise:

1) **Put your *raison d'être* in the middle.** Then everything else can come outwards from that, like a spider diagram. After all the thinking you've done so far, choose the one overriding most important thing that drives you in your life. The one thing that matters more than anything else. I discovered years ago that mine is simply sustainable happiness – both for my family and for me. What brings happiness, of course, then needs to be understood, but at the end of the day, as long as my family and I are happy, that's what counts most for me at the moment. It could be your children, becoming prime minister, your health, your relationship, winning an Olympic gold medal, making a million, helping others, being the best

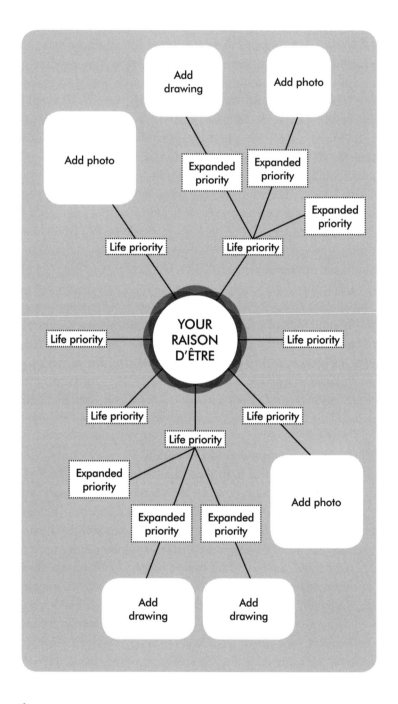

person you can be. It may well change through life also. My 16-year-old self would certainly have said the sole purpose of my life was being the slalom canoeing world champion.

2) **Make sure the other things you capture support your *raison d'être* and, or, touch you deeply.** So, I have captured things that make me happy and content in a sustainable way and that help to make my family happy – the things in which I want to invest time and energy. In addition, I have put on the key values around the person that I want to be. Only capture on your Lifeboard the **things that really matter.** Nothing should be on there that you don't see or feel as being a really key element or driver in your life.

3) **Don't choose too many.** Ideally, I think you want between four and eight life priorities. You can expand on these areas, though, if it helps you convey what you want to, as shown in the diagram to the left. For example, one of your life priorities could be family and you could expand that out with specifics such as 'partner', 'children', 'parents'. Or you could put each of these as a separate life priority in their own right; in mine I have put my relationship with my partner, my children, and my family (which includes my parents and my brother and his family) as three separate life priorities.

The diagram to the left is just an example – you can follow this type of template if you want to, expanding each of the life priorities out if you like and not if you don't. But feel free to disregard this and create your Lifeboard in whatever way works for you. I would suggest a starting point would be to get a blank piece of A3 paper and just try capturing your initial thoughts either in written words, pictures or a diagram. From there you can decide how you want to present your Lifeboard.

ALIGN YOUR LIFE TO WHAT MATTERS

The next step is to reflect on all of this. If this is what's really important to you, how has that informed (or not) your life choices so far? Is the path you are currently treading through life reflective of this? Are there choices you could make going forwards that will align your life more closely to this? What would aligning your life behind your priorities look like?

Even though you are now clearer about your life priorities, the implications of these will be different for everyone. For example, once I had children I decided that family was my priority and therefore I would work part-time, clearly earning less money as a result and potentially risking a negative impact on my career, so that I could spend more time with my children.

However, I remember a very young, high-flying senior vice president with a European remit with whom I worked who had the same priority (his family) but made very different decisions as a result. He had a day of holiday booked because it was his son's birthday party. Unfortunately, on that day a meeting was arranged with the new CEO, his new boss, for the whole leadership team. He cancelled his day off and attended the meeting. At the time I was, shall we say, less than impressed. It certainly wasn't the choice I would have made and I would have said that was because I put my family first.

When I got to know him better, though, I understood he absolutely believed in family first. Nothing was more important to him than the wellbeing of his wife and children. The role he saw for him in that equation though was, in his words, "wealth creation for my family". That was how he translated the value he added to his family – the more successful he was, the more money he earned, the more opportunity he believed he created for his family. It was a key meeting with the new CEO and from a career perspective attending it was very important indeed. The underlying driver for him still, though, despite not going to his son's birthday party, was his family. It was his interpretation of 'putting his family first'.

I've seen people make so many different types of choices to get their lives more aligned behind what really matters to them. There are, of course, still traditional family set-ups where the male is the main breadwinner and the female the stay-at-home family carer and, for many families, that may be exactly the set-up that works for them.

But there are also lots of examples out there of people making different choices about how their lives are organized. There's the obvious part-time working or job-share to allow parents to spend more time with children, but I also know a very inspiring individual who has changed from working five days to four days a week in order to spend the fifth day volunteering at the Prince's Trust. I know a number of men who've taken sabbaticals or time off to spend more time with their family as well as a number of executive-level women who are the 'lead career' in their relationship and are supported by their stay-at-home husbands who are the main child-carers on an ongoing basis.

I know couples who have left their jobs to set up businesses together to enable them to create control and flexibility over their work and life; examples of this range from creating a consultancy to running a chocolate shop. A good friend of mine, having worked for a number of years as a skilled and successful primary school teacher, decided to leave the school she worked at and teach on a supply basis. This allows her to continue teaching, which she loves, but gives her more flexibility in her life, which she wanted.

I know an accountant who works very long hours when he is working on key deals, but in between those, he takes a lot of time back and is often with his wife and son in the daytime.

I recently met a parent who talked about how she and her husband both do contract work. Salaries for non-permanent contracts tend to be higher and they are in the fortunate position where they can live on one or the other's salary. They take a 'drop in' and 'drop out' approach – sometimes they both have contracts and at other times just one or other of them will so that they can each fulfil various family and life responsibilities at different points.

I realize not everyone will be in the same financial position, but the more I meet people and talk to them about how they set up their lives, the more options and possibilities I discover are out there. It's about finding the one that works for you, your family and your priorities.

You may be thinking I am making this all sound very easy – now you know your life priorities so off you go and align your life choices behind it, all sorted. Clearly, I realize it is not as simple as that. There will inevitably be implications and consequences of any choice you make. Here comes the question: can anyone have it all? Well, in my opinion, that is simply a matter of logic and interpretation. If having it all means:

WORKING FULL-TIME AND LONG HOURS IN ORDER TO MAXIMIZE YOUR CHANCES OF PROMOTION THEREBY GETTING INTO THAT VERY SENIOR JOB AS QUICKLY AS POSSIBLE WHICH MEETS YOUR HIGH NEED FOR ACHIEVEMENT, AND AS A RESULT EARNING LOADS OF MONEY, AND AT THE SAME TIME GETTING TO SPEND LOTS OF QUALITY TIME WITH YOUR FAMILY, AND GOING TO THE GYM REGULARLY, CONTINUING TO GET DOWN THE PUB WITH YOUR MATES AND CATCHING THE LATEST FILM RELEASES WHILST THEY'RE STILL AT THE CINEMA

… then you haven't got a chance.

If having it all can be defined as:

GETTING THE THINGS OUT OF LIFE THAT ARE MOST IMPORTANT TO YOU, ACCEPTING THE IMPLICATIONS ON OTHER AREAS OF YOUR LIFE (BECAUSE THEY ARE A RESULT OF PRIORITY DECISIONS YOU ARE MAKING YOURSELF), SO THAT YOU FEEL YOU'RE GETTING JUST ENOUGH FROM THOSE OTHER AREAS TO MEET YOUR RECONCILED NEEDS

… then I think you can be on to a winner.

The point is, we have to be realistic and we have to accept the consequences of our choices. Consequences don't mean the choices are wrong, they simply mean there are 24 hours in a day and seven days in a week and at some point we all need to get some sleep.

I have had to accept the implications of being a gay parent, for example. As an employee in a global company, my career opportunities have at times been limited by both my family and my life choices. The more senior you become, the greater the expectation that you are willing to relocate internationally, in order both to build your international experience and to have the greatest number of roles available to you as potential next steps.

Being married to a woman, particularly with two children, however, can make the world feel very small indeed. According to the International Lesbian and Gay Association's worldwide legislation information on its website (www.ilga.org) there are still five countries and parts of Nigeria and Somalia where being gay is punishable by death. There are more than 40 countries in Africa and Asia where being gay is illegal, and large parts of the world where there is no legal protection whatsoever, so you could be fired for being gay and that would be legal.

Clearly, I would certainly not take my family to live in any of these countries. Sadly there are still only 13 countries in the world that afford gay people equal marriage rights. This limits my career opportunities.

In addition to this, as a result of the holistic approach I take to life, I have never been someone who works long hours. When I'm at work, I'm completely committed to delivering everything and more than is expected of me, but I also want time outside work to pursue my other interests. I see other people who started working at the same age as me, who are now significantly more senior than I am, usually men as it happens, and I see that they work quite a few more hours than me over the course of the weeks and months. This frustrates me, of course, because I am every bit as smart and talented as them (or so my mum tells me), and I could argue I add more value to the business because of the vibrancy and energy I bring to work as a result of my holistic life.

But I certainly wouldn't want to swap my life for theirs; no way. They can keep their bigger jobs and bigger pay cheques, and I'll hold on to my quality time with my family, my tennis matches and my undisturbed holidays and weekends, thank you. It's just a shame that it has to be a choice at the moment. I believe our society will get past this, but we're not there yet and so we need to make our choices.

KEEP IT FRONT OF MIND

The final critical point about your Lifeboard is that you need to keep it alive! It is so very easy to do all this work and thinking and then forget about it next week. Find the way that allows you to keep it front of mind. Visual reminders work for me – I'm very 'out of sight, out of mind'. I don't want my Lifeboard on the wall at home – that would be a bit embarrassing – so I put it on the inside of my wardrobe door. That way, every morning when I get dressed, I see it and remember what's important to me. I know other people who've had key rings made with photos, or made their Lifeboard into a mouse mat! Whatever works for you. Sharing it with others can help, I find. But make sure you do something to keep it at the forefront of your mind because otherwise, I guarantee, next month, if not before, you will not be making choices aligned to this and your life priorities will be back in the important-but-not-urgent box.

BE *(absolutely)* FABULOUS

CHAPTER

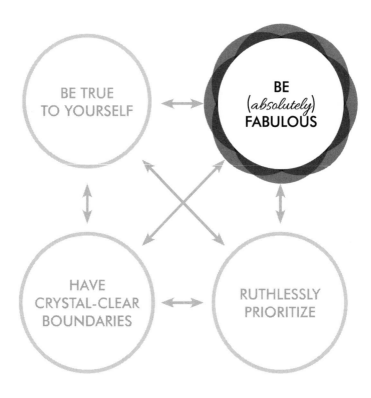

CHAPTER 3

BE *(absolutely)* FABULOUS

WE ALL GET DRAGGED DOWN SOMETIMES

Modern life is fast-paced, stressful and can feel relentless. Every now and then, I think this can get to us all, and we can have periods when we feel ground down. Even if you love where you work, it can still be hard to get up and go every day. Even if you love your job, there will inevitably be parts of it in which you are less interested, at best. Some people are in the unfortunate position of not enjoying their job or are perpetually unhappy with something about it – for example, their boss, the stress or the long hours. Having off days occasionally, feeling grumpy, being distracted or less engaged are simply factors of life. The key word here, though,

is 'occasionally'. It can be so easy to slip into negative thoughts, habits and behaviours, and focus on what's not so great rather than the things that are positive.

And in my experience there are always positives, as long as you look for them.

The point is not only that it's essentially not very nice to feel negative or down but, critically, that the people who are at their best are more likely to get the best opportunities. In my experience, it's very unusual for the people who are not in a positive place, who lack enthusiasm or who are dissatisfied with something about their work or life to be perceived as the 'best people'. Sometimes people get so ground down at work you can practically see a black cloud over their heads. Even if there's good reason for this, for example, they may be having a difficult time outside work, it doesn't change the fact that it's easy to be perceived as not committed and a less good performer. Despite the fact that life has ups and downs, we all need to find a way to be the best we can be, no matter what we are doing, how we're doing it or who we're doing it with.

A lot of organizations focus on employee engagement, and rightly so. The more interested they can get their employees in what they are doing and why, the more each will contribute. But it's not just the responsibility of the organization, nor is it just for the benefit of the organization, for each of us to be firing on all cylinders. If you think about the days at work you've enjoyed the most I would bet they are days when you've achieved things, been productive and felt positive. Every individual has to take responsibility for this themselves.

CAN WE LEARN ANYTHING FROM SPORT?
There's been a trend for a number of years of bringing Olympic athletes or sports coaches into workplaces to draw parallels between sporting achievements and work success. I have to admit, I

was pretty cynical about this to start with. As I said in the introduction, I was a member of the Great Britain Junior Canoe Slalom Team, and captained that team to the World Championships. Sport was my life. I trained 12 times a week and had posters on my wall that said things like

WHEN YOU ARE NOT TRAINING, SOMEONE, SOMEWHERE IS, AND WHEN YOU MEET, SHE WILL WIN

or

FAILING TO PREPARE IS PREPARING TO FAIL

Let's just say I was pretty intensely focused and it was all for the love of the sport, the competition and the winning. I wasn't earning any money for it, it was all purely driven by intrinsic motivation. The lows were pretty tough – breaking the ice on the local pond to train on a winter morning before college or just missing out on that all-important Junior World Championship medal in my last year as an under-18. But the highs were incredible – winning the British Junior Championships or the Junior European 'Europa Cup' Championship. So when someone turned up at my workplace and started to tell me that my doing some PowerPoint slides, going to meetings or helping someone give feedback in a constructive way had parallels to elite sport, I didn't buy it.

Interestingly though, as the years go by, I see more and more connections between the two. Not so much between things I do at work and racing at the World Championships, but more the ability sports people have to sustain incredibly high levels of performance, dedication, energy and focus, relentlessly, for years and years without burning out. Constantly reinventing themselves and finding new ways to be even better at what they are doing. The ability to perform exceptionally at exactly the time they need to. In short, the ability to bring out the best in ourselves consistently is, in fact, similar in sport and at work.

There, I've said it. I admit it. And now that I have admitted it, the idea of thriving in the workplace feels a bit more exciting, and quite frankly, a little bit more heroic.

BEING IN THE ZONE

If we accept there is plenty to learn from sport that can help us be the best we can be in a sustainable way, we can start to borrow excellent expressions like 'being in the zone'! This is described in *The Free Dictionary* by Farlex (www.freedictionary.com) as being "in a state of focused attention or energy so that one's performance is enhanced". In the context of work, I would say this is effectively those days or times when it all comes together and you feel like you are on fire (in a good way) – you are totally focused and everything you do is extra effective. It's a positive place.

Being 'in the zone' as much as you can be is absolutely the aim. Realistically, sustaining this level of performance for long periods is not possible. What is realistic is sustaining positive, focused, effective and efficient ways of working, meaning you are being the best you can be, all the time. This will look and feel different for everyone and certainly the circumstances that create this will be personal to you. To thrive, some people want clear direction, others autonomy, some want to work alone, others with colleagues, some want pressure, others want time, some need a purpose, others just want a goal. It's not important what the circumstances are in which you thrive, it's only important to know them.

To try and understand how you make this your norm it's important to understand when you have felt this way. Think about a time when you've enjoyed your job the most, you've been most successful, you've had the most energy – a time when you feel that you were in, or as close as possible to being in, 'the zone'. You could be thinking about a day, an afternoon even, a particular meeting, a week, or a longer period of time. Once you have this in mind, consider the circumstances and context and capture the key things that you think enabled this situation here:

WHEN I WAS IN THE ZONE IT WAS ENABLED BY:

Answering the following questions will help to flush this out further:

WHAT ARE THE FIVE OR SO WORDS YOU WOULD USE
TO DESCRIBE THIS TIME?

....

....

WHAT WERE THE CIRCUMSTANCES?

....

....

....

WHAT WAS THE ENVIRONMENT LIKE?

....

....

WHAT DID YOU LOVE THE MOST ABOUT THIS TIME AND WHY?

....

....

....

HOW DID YOU FEEL?

....

....

WHY DID YOU FEEL THIS WAY?

....

....

WHAT WERE THE RELATIONSHIPS YOU HAD LIKE?

....

....

ON A SCALE OF 1-10 (1 BEING NONE AND 10 BEING LOADS):

HOW MUCH SUPPORT DID YOU HAVE? ....

HOW MUCH DIRECTION DID YOU HAVE? ....

HOW MUCH AUTONOMY DID YOU HAVE? ....

HOW WOULD YOU DESCRIBE YOUR MANAGER?

....

....

WHAT ELSE CAN YOU REMEMBER ABOUT THIS TIME?

....

....

WHAT WAS GOING ON OUTSIDE WORK THAT
MAY HAVE HAD AN IMPACT?

....

....

Now do the opposite. Sorry to drag up bad memories, but it's equally important to understand the circumstances in which you do not thrive. Think about a time when you least enjoyed your job, when you were less successful and you had less energy. Once you have this in mind, consider the circumstances and context as you did before, and make notes to capture the key things that you think created this situation here:

WHEN I WAS NOT IN THE ZONE IT WAS BECAUSE:

Try answering the same questions again from the perspective of not being in the zone or on top form:

WHAT ARE THE FIVE OR SO WORDS YOU WOULD USE
TO DESCRIBE THIS TIME?

....

....

WHAT WERE THE CIRCUMSTANCES?

....

....

....

WHAT WAS THE ENVIRONMENT LIKE?

....

....

WHAT DID YOU LOVE THE MOST ABOUT THIS TIME AND WHY?

....

....

....

HOW DID YOU FEEL?

....

....

WHY DID YOU FEEL THIS WAY?

....

....

WHAT WERE THE RELATIONSHIPS YOU HAD LIKE?

....

....

ON A SCALE OF 1–10 (1 BEING NONE AND 10 BEING LOADS):

HOW MUCH SUPPORT DID YOU HAVE? ....

HOW MUCH DIRECTION DID YOU HAVE? ....

HOW MUCH AUTONOMY DID YOU HAVE? ....

HOW WOULD YOU DESCRIBE YOUR MANAGER?

....

....

WHAT ELSE CAN YOU REMEMBER ABOUT THIS TIME?

....

....

WHAT WAS GOING ON OUTSIDE WORK THAT
MAY HAVE HAD AN IMPACT?

....

....

Now you should have a good understanding of the types of factor that enable you to be at your best and those that stand in your way. Summarize them in the following table; ignore the 'control/influence' column for now, I'll come on to that later.

Factors that enable me to be in the zone	Control/ Influence	Factors that inhibit me from being in the zone	Control/ Influence

The next step is to understand which of these are in your control and which are not. For this, I refer to a tool of Stephen R. Covey's from *The 7 Habits of Highly Effective People* called the Spheres of Influence and Control.

This tool allows you to consider whether a factor is fully in your control, something that you can influence, or something over which you have no control. This is important to understand because it becomes clear which things we need just to accept and on which we should try to put a positive spin, and the things about which we can do something. Sometimes things we assume are out of our control actually end up being things we can change. Go back to your list of factors that enable and inhibit you from being in the zone and note down in the 'control/influence' column for each one whether it's:

- In your **control**; for example, what time of day you do certain types of work, such as checking emails or writing a proposal; or your energy levels in relation to sleep and exercise.
- Something you can **influence;** for example, the amount of direction or autonomy you receive could be influenced by a conversation with your line manager.
- Something **outside your control**; for example, if your line manager is incompetent or you dislike your colleagues.

How much you travel in your role might be something that you perceive to be outside your control. However, it could be that if you suggested a way of working differently, such as having meetings less frequently or meeting virtually with Skype, but sharing information more regularly through forums or portals making better use of technology, you could influence this. You may have been told you can't drop your working days to three from five, but perhaps if you proactively found a willing job-share partner and went to your manager with a workable solution to cover all five days between you, that could make a difference.

For everything you identified as being within your control or within your sphere of influence, consider what actions you could take to align your day-to-day reality with being the best you can be. For those things out of your control, you need to use the power of positive thought, which I will come on to later in this chapter.

I will also explore other areas within your control that can help to create the circumstances you require to thrive and to enable you to consistently be the best you can be.

UNDERSTANDING YOUR ENERGY

Managing energy levels is key to leading a productive, effective and fun life. We all naturally have energy highs and lows throughout the day and what we decide to do in relation to exercise, activity and diet can have an enormous impact on this.

First, it's important to understand this natural pattern of energy and how it fluctuates. It is driven by our circadian rhythms, which are defined by the National Institute of General Medical Sciences on their *Circadian Rhythms Fact Sheet* (www.nigms.nih. gov) as "physical, mental and behavioural changes that follow a roughly 24-hour cycle, responding primarily to light and darkness in an organism's environment". These rhythms impact our sleep–wake cycles, our hormone levels and our body temperature. In short, they impact our energy levels. When you understand your rhythm, you can, if possible, plan the type of activity you do at particular times of the day and proactively manage slumps in energy. Over the course of a normal day, my energy levels would look something like this:

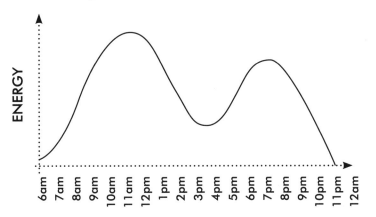

As a result of this I know that the late mornings are my most productive time and so work that involves a great deal of concentration, or is very important, I do then. I also know that I have an energy slump early afternoon.

I once had a global conference call at 3pm – right when my energy is lowest. In addition, I was eight-months pregnant at the time. I was the only attendee from the UK and was sitting in a meeting room in the office on my own; I dialled in to the call on a conference phone on loudspeaker. I had been on the call a while when suddenly the phone broke! The line just went completely dead and started making a long monotone 'beeping' sound.

Then it dawned on me, the phone hadn't broken at all, the meeting was over – I'd fallen asleep!

I'd actually fallen asleep, with my head on the desk, and completely missed the end of the call. The phone line had gone dead because everyone else had hung up. I still, to this day, do not know if anyone said on that call "Claire, any questions or input from the UK?". Let's hope not.

As a result, I have since learned that if I do some exercise at lunchtime – go for a run, to the gym, or even just for a walk in the fresh air – and have a light lunch, this slump is significantly less. It is also clear that working late into the evening does not work very well for me. My energy levels, and therefore concentration, drop and I tend to make more mistakes than I would during the day. Not a good time to do detailed work. I realize not everyone has autonomy over what they do or when. But even if you can't change the time of activities during your day, being aware of your natural rhythm can help you to manage your energy highs and lows.

Think about your own natural rhythm and plot on the chart opposite how you think your energy levels change during a 24-hour period.

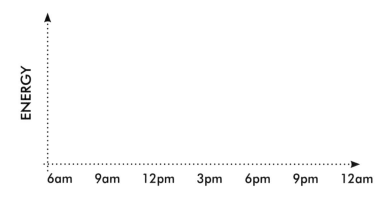

Reflect on your energy levels throughout a normal day and consider the following questions to help shape your thoughts:

WHAT DO YOU NOTICE ABOUT YOUR ENERGY LEVELS DURING THE DAY?

....

....

....

....

WHEN ARE YOUR ENERGY LEVELS HIGHEST?

....

....

....

....

WHEN ARE THEY LOWEST?

....

....

....

....

COULD YOU MAKE DIFFERENT CHOICES ABOUT WHAT ACTIVITIES OR WORK YOU DO AT PARTICULAR TIMES?

....

DO YOU HAVE STRATEGIES TO ACTIVELY MANAGE YOUR ENERGY LEVELS?

....

WE ARE WHAT WE EAT

One of the best ways of managing energy levels is through what and when we eat and drink. We all know how incredibly sleepy we feel in the afternoon after a large roast dinner, especially when accompanied by a few glasses of wine. By contrast, we can also see the short-term energy hit gained from caffeine and sugar. For proof of this, give a toddler some chocolate and then watch them go! The impact is almost instant; it's like a wind-up toy.

These short-term energy highs are often followed by the lows of a large Sunday roast, though. We need to avoid the cycle of feeling energy lows, giving ourselves a sugar or caffeine hit to perk up, then, as a result, experiencing another energy low after a period and needing more sugar or caffeine to pick us up. The trick is to try to maintain energy at a relatively consistent level. Basically, the starting point is to eat a healthy diet. Get your five portions of fruit and veg a day (I used to think this was actually impossible but it really is pretty straight forward if you give your meals and snacks some forethought) and exclude, or at least limit, processed and high-fat or high-sugar foods.

In addition, some tops tips are:

- Eat protein such as yoghurt or egg as part of a well-balanced breakfast as this helps to keep hunger at bay.
- Eat a healthy snack mid-morning and mid-afternoon, or when you feel you are having an energy dip between meals, such as nuts and raisins, fruit or toast with honey.
- Treat yourself to a tea or coffee if you fancy it, but limit how many cups you have a day.
- Manage your portion size rather than having large meals.

PHYSICAL ACTIVITY SAVES YOUR LIFE

There is overwhelming evidence to show that regular moderate physical activity makes you live longer. An article on the BBC news website (www.bbc.co.uk) headlined *Inactivity 'kills more than obesity'* by James Gallagher (15 January 2015), reported that "A lack of exercise could be killing twice as many people as obesity in Europe". Physical activity also has a profound impact on our energy levels as well as our ability to manage stress. If you're in a sedentary job, just getting up every 20 minutes – particularly at times you are expecting your energy to drop – and walking, even just to get a drink, can be enough to maintain a greater level of concentration and energy. Consider the simple things you could do differently to be more active:

- **Walk more:** get your own coffee or water; use the stairs not the lift; walk to people in your office to speak to them rather than phoning or messaging them; walk to a local café once a day to treat yourself to a cuppa; park at the far side of car park; get off the bus a couple of stops early; walk around the block during a break.

I used to think that the Holy Grail of health of achieving 20 minutes of brisk walking per day didn't apply to me because, three times a week, I trained really hard at the gym. In the face of overwhelming evidence, I have had to accept that if I want to live longer I still need to do 20 minutes of brisk walking a day, in addition, because my daily life is so sedentary. My gym work keeps me fit, but it doesn't give the benefits of consistent daily moderate physical activity that are so important.

- **Sitting down is over-rated:** we do it for hours at a time. We sit down to work, to eat, to have a coffee, to watch TV, and the long and short of it is it's not good for us. Try standing more. On the bus or train, when chatting to people, particularly if you're on the phone, and in meetings.

When I am finding it hard to keep my concentration in a meeting I stand up. It is possible people think I'm a bit odd for it but I don't care, it significantly improves my focus and concentration, it stops big energy dips and it quite simply helps me live longer – what's weird in wanting that? Some workplaces have standing desks that are higher than usual so that you can stand and work at your computer, some even have treadmill desks allowing you to walk and type at the same time. I can see some potential flaws with this though…

In one of my global roles I had the pleasure of working for a boss who was both knowledgeable and passionate about health and fitness. For a period, we both tried sitting on a stability ball (the large inflatable balls you find in gyms to do core abdominal work on) at our desks instead of a chair. We wobbled around together at our computers feeling happy that, while working, we were also developing our core strength! It was great, but we did find that we could only sit on the balls for short periods of time without it becoming uncomfortable. The problem was, when we swapped back to our chairs for a break, the balls had a mind of their own. They used to roll off around the office bumping into other people, and sometimes tripping them up, so unfortunately our grand plan didn't last long. When I look back on it now I think we could have easily come up with a way of stopping them rolling off if we'd thought it through properly.

Consider how long you sit at your desk, and try and plan to get up every 20 minutes to walk around the room, at least. Try it for a day and notice the difference it makes.

- **Take more breaks:** taking regular breaks helps us to maintain our concentration and energy. Just getting away from your screen and having a change of scene is beneficial.

I know individuals who read a book for half-an-hour at lunchtime to get a bit of quiet time, and people who have a little group who go for a walk around the block together. Make sure at least mid-afternoon and ideally mid-morning, as well as at lunchtime, you stop working and take a short rest. This is a great time to employ some of the relaxation and mindfulness techniques I will come to later, or you can simply try doing something different for ten minutes – a change is as good as a rest, they say!

Moderate activity aside, it is also of significant value to make more rigorous regular sport or exercise part of your weekly routine. In a busy life, with a full-on job and family responsibilities, it can feel impossible to find the opportunity to fit in the gym, a run, play a sport or whatever it is you would like to do. But these things are critical to our health, happiness, stress levels, fitness and wellbeing. In my experience, there's always a way as long as you're committed to finding it.

Different things work for different people. Some people like the regular commitment of team sports like five-a-side football, or going to a running club, others like the flexibility of fitting in a run or a swim when it suits them. I know not everyone is naturally into exercise, but if you want to keep fit, have energy, beat stress, lose weight or experience a natural high you literally can't beat it. I know lots of people who evangelize about the benefits of exercise and fitness having got into it later in life. I don't know anyone who has regretted it. So here are some top tips:

1) **Do what you enjoy the most**. If you hate running try swimming; if you can't motivate yourself to exercise alone, arrange to meet a friend; if you enjoy watching sport then play sport; if you're worried joining a gym will be a waste of money find a gym where you can pay per session. Find out what's happening locally – there are lots of classes in the parks these days like boot camps or circuits that you can join.

2) **Have a goal**. Something to aim for and work towards is key as it gives you focus and motivation. This could be entering a race or competition, doing a parkrun, getting a programme created for you, setting your own weight loss or fitness goal. It doesn't matter what it is as long as it's something you can strive for.

3) **Plan it in**. I know not everyone is a planner, but the reality of busy lives is that the peripheral things get dropped. Make it a core part of your week. On a Sunday night, think about the one or two or even three times in the week when you will fit in some exercise. Put it in the diary. Stick to it.

4) **Do it with other people**. It's always easier to follow through when you are making a commitment to someone else as well as yourself. You don't even necessarily need to exercise together, if it's not possible. But find someone who wants to start being more active too, share your plans, and then catch up regularly

on how you're getting on. You'll find it's harder to skip a session when you'll have to confess it to someone else.

You may have to be a bit creative about finding opportunities. Over the years I have done it in various different ways depending on my circumstances at the time. For example:

- Running or walking to or from work is a great way to combine a functional commute with getting exercise. If the journey is too long, get the train or bus and then get off halfway there.
- Running or using the gym before, during or after work. There is a brilliant trend at the moment for short but intense 30-minute exercise classes that are much easier to fit in during the day.
- Doing things that involve the family; when my children were small, I did buggy fit classes, and also used to go running with one of them in the buggy. You could also cycle together, run while the kids cycle, run or cycle whilst walking the dog, go swimming or walking together.
- Exercise early or late. At the moment, to exercise at the weekend I tend to get up and out first thing to get it done without it impacting the day or my having the opportunity to lose my motivation. I know other people who go late, after the children are in bed, for example.
- Exercise at home. Exercise videos or following an exercise app can be a good way to motivate yourself to exercise at home because it gives you some direction. Sometimes the kids 'help' me with my home exercise by sitting on my back while I'm trying to do press-ups or 'the plank'.
- Exercise on 'work-from-home' days. If you're in a job where you can work from home that's a perfect opportunity to have a regular exercise slot. I used to run at lunchtime because it broke the day up and felt good to get out of the house, but now I drop the children at nursery in my running kit and go straight out because I prefer to get it done.

My children are too young to cycle while I run but I'm hoping when they are a bit older they will sometimes want to do that. Then maybe we can run together when they're older still. Then, slightly depressingly I suppose, in the end, I'll have to cycle while they run in order to keep up. But that's ok, that's the point – you have to evolve and change how you fit things in depending on your circumstances. You have to be a bit flexible and creative to make it work.

If childcare is a barrier for you, try to find a friend with children you could put a reciprocal babysitting arrangement in place with – they have the kids while you exercise, then swap. Personal training can also be a great way to get motivated and get new ideas on what to do. I realize it costs money but even if you just have one or two sessions a month or even a year it can be enough to give you that extra drive and motivation that you need.

MAKE WORK FUN

You can always spice up a tough or mundane day by setting yourself little challenges. For example, getting a certain amount of work done in a particular amount of time, or perhaps before another person. One summer between academic years at university, a group of friends and I worked in a factory. Our job was to unpack boxes of product, stack them up on pallets, and then shrink-wrap the pallets to be picked up by the forklift truck driver, who, I was pleased to see, was a woman.

This could have made for very boring long days. Being relentlessly competitive though, my friends and I suggested to the supervisor that if we split into two teams and worked on two pallets at once we could get more pallets packed in less time. We then, of course, raced each other. This made it an awful lot more fun, so we enjoyed it, and the supervisor was happy because we got a lot more pallets stacked. I think that's called a win–win situation.

DOES IT REALLY MATTER IF THE GLASS IS HALF-FULL OR HALF-EMPTY?

Positivity is a choice. We all choose every day and at every moment how we interpret what happens around us. What is critical to understand is that it's all about perspective. If you asked Patsy and Eddie from the, quite frankly hilarious, comedy show *Absolutely Fabulous* whether a glass was half-full or half-empty I suspect their reply would be something along the lines of:

"Who bloody cares, just fill it up again!"

Interpreting a glass as half-empty is classically seen as being negative, but I challenge that. I had the unfortunate experience of a barium follow-through X-ray once. Effectively, this involves drinking a large quantity of metallic fluid and then being X-rayed periodically to track it as it moves through your intestines. I can tell you that barium is disgusting and managing to interpret that large glass as being 'half-empty' as opposed to 'half-full' at the earliest point possible was a huge feat of positivity.

If we're going to go with clichés, I prefer "every cloud has a silver lining", and I really believe this is true. We need to find the positives in our everyday life. Try an exercise I call 5 x 2. This is simply thinking five positive thoughts, twice a day.

5 x 2: EVENING REFLECTIONS

During the evening, take time to reflect on your day. I do this when I'm in bed just before I go to sleep, but it can be earlier if you prefer. I go through my whole day and think about the five most positive things that have happened. The important part here is relativity. I'm not looking for five positive things, but the five **most** positive things. This means that even if you've had a tough day and it's hard to find things about which you are happy, you still need to challenge yourself to find the things that were better than the really bad bits. On a great day, the five could be:

1) Playing a fun game of 'hide and seek' with the children
2) Doing a brilliant exercise class
3) Getting offered an amazing job
4) Eating at an excellent restaurant to celebrate your new job
5) Getting an 'early night' with your loved one

On a tough, busy or stressful day you will need to dig deeper to find the positives, and they could be things like:

1) Bumping into someone at the coffee machine who you like
2) Making a joke in your meeting that people found funny
3) Someone unexpectedly offering to make you a cup of tea
4) Enjoying a glass nice glass of wine at the end of the day
5) Catching the last half an hour of *MasterChef*

I find that, when going through my day, I have often forgotten some of the little things that happened. Just reflecting on them and pulling out the nicest parts of your day, even if they are small things, means you go to sleep at night with a positive perspective.

5 x 2: THE DAY AHEAD

I used to find it difficult to drag myself out of bed in the mornings, so I started trying this and it worked a treat. After the alarm goes off, but before the snooze reminds me not to go back to sleep I think about the five things I am looking forward to most about the day. Again it could be big or small things depending on the day, but on average it looks something like this:

1) Having a coffee and snuggle with the kids on the couch before going to work when they are still all sleepy, cuddly and incredibly cute (they drink milk, I drink the coffee)
2) Seeing a particular person whose company I enjoy, either at work or socially
3) Going to the gym, running or playing tennis
4) Something that I'm going to achieve, perhaps work that I'm delivering or a book that I will finish reading that day
5) Having dinner with my partner and catching up on our days

It's not rocket science, but it means that the thoughts in your head when you drag your tired self reluctantly out of bed (or is that just me?) are positive ones focused on the things in the day to which you are looking forward, rather than negative ones about having to get out of your comfortable bed – for example, it's cold, the trains will be busy, you're feeling tired.

I realize that, for many people with children, the reality of the mornings is a bit different to that which I've described. If only the kids would not wake you up before the time the alarm is supposed to go off! I've been woken up far too early many times by my two boys bouncing into our room, climbing on the bed, sitting on my head (sometimes with full nappies), prising my eyes open with their fingers and, on seeing me snuggled up in bed trying to sleep, exclaiming "Mummy, what <u>are</u> you doing?" as if trying to be asleep at 5.30am is the most unreasonable thing in the world. On these mornings, I just go with the flow, but if I'm feeling negative or grumpy, I soon remember to think about the five things I am most looking forward to that day – sometimes it's just bedtime!

DECIDING TO BE POSITIVE

Simply deciding to be positive is surprisingly effective. A couple of years ago, my partner and I went on a three-night snowboarding holiday, without our children, with four of our best friends.

We were extremely excited about it and so much wanted to have an amazing time. On the way to the airport, I told my partner that I had decided, no matter what happened on this holiday, I wasn't going to let anything bother me or annoy me, I was just going to have an amazing time. Now, you could claim that was asking for trouble… and perhaps unsurprisingly quite a few things went wrong. My snowboard was not put on our plane, the roads to the resort were shut due to heavy snowfall, the hire car did not come with the snow-chains we had booked, and the night before leaving to come home the snowfall was so heavy we were very concerned about the possibility of not making it back to the airport in time.

Incredibly, however, I took all this in my stride. Nothing bothered me, I found the positives, I was pragmatic and I didn't let myself get worried about the 'what ifs…'. I have no doubt whatsoever that, had I not have made the commitment to myself and to my partner about not letting anything spoil my holiday, I would have been stressed out, annoyed, upset and worried. This not only would have been unpleasant for me but it wouldn't have been much fun for those around me either. Just by having made that commitment, I was able to look at things in a different, more positive light, to reframe what was happening to see the opportunities and choices.

I am not saying we could live every day like this because it did take commitment and focus, but it certainly goes to show that how we react to and interpret what happens to us and around us is very much in our control.

Keeping a positive mindset is particularly important if you are presenting some work in a meeting, speaking at an event, in a job interview, or at a pivotal point in a big project. Sometimes, if you perceive someone's reaction to be negative, it can knock your confidence and impact your behaviour unfavourably.

I will never forget the first time I presented an HR strategy to a board of business leaders. I had done my homework, or so I thought. I had got input from all the functional heads, diligently covering marketing, sales, finance, and the managing director in pre-meetings, to get their buy-in and commitment so that when I presented at the leadership team session it would be a slam-dunk of a sign-off. At the meeting, however, things took a turn for the worse. One of my key stakeholders looked surprised at what I was sharing right from the start. It really threw me because I had thought she was aligned and now, at this late hour, she had her eyebrows raised at everything I was proposing. I tried hard to keep my composure, but I couldn't avoid the negative thoughts in my head in reaction to her behaviour and I stumbled through the rest of my presentation decidedly less professionally than I had intended.

Afterwards, I shared my concerns with another leadership team colleague saying how disappointed and concerned I was about this particular team member's surprise, and she responded by saying:

OH, DON'T WORRY ABOUT HER, SHE WASN'T RAISING HER EYEBROWS BECAUSE SHE WAS SURPRISED, SHE JUST HAD BOTOX THIS MORNING!

It's critical to believe in yourself, even in the face of adversity. Try the following:

Every time you notice yourself having a negative thought about yourself, what you're doing, or how someone feels about you or is behaving towards you, force yourself to think two positive thoughts: one to neutralize the negative thought and one to tip the balance to positivity. It's up to you what your positive thoughts are. I find it works well if the first one is in relation to the negative thought you had – reframing it into something positive, as shown in the examples below, but the second one could just be any old frivolous positive thought – something you're looking forward to, something great you've done or something nice someone did for you or said to you.

NEGATIVE THOUGHT	FINDING THE POSITIVE
I'm scared my presentation won't go well	In just 30 minutes the presentation will be over and whatever happens, I will be a better presenter for having had the experience
John made a comment to me that wasn't nice and it annoyed and upset me	I rose above it and did not respond despite the fact that it upset me – I'm proud of myself for doing that
I'm not capable of doing what I've been asked	I have a proven track record of delivering, they are demonstrating faith in me by asking me and it's an opportunity to stretch myself

Decide to be positive today, and tomorrow and the next day.

MINDFULNESS AND MEDITATION

Learn to relax instantly and get a grip of our thoughts whenever we want. Who wouldn't want that?

We have focused already on the value of being 'present' (remember the biscuit story?) and being in the moment. This is the basis for mindfulness. Mindfulness is an ancient Buddhist practice and is simply about paying attention in the present moment, on purpose, in a non-judgmental way. It is well-proven to reduce anxiety and combat stress.

This may sound simple, and in concept, it is. But in our everyday lives it is incredibly easy to be distracted – not to pay full attention to what we are doing. Mindfulness helps to enable us to constantly live in the present moment and notice the little things.

It is very similar to basic meditation, which involves learning to relax, quickly and consciously, and to control your thoughts or pay attention. Whichever approach you prefer, if practised, will bring about significant health and wellbeing benefits, particularly helping with reducing stress and anxiety. Reconnecting with our inner selves and enabling attention to our thoughts can be as simple as sitting for five minutes somewhere quiet and focusing on your breathing. To start with, I recommend following some instruction as these are skills that, once mastered, are simple and quick to apply at most points in the day, but initially take time to learn and understand.

To get a feel for it, try this simple breathing exercise that helps to clear your mind and relax you and can be done easily at any point in the day:

- Sit or lie somewhere quiet and comfortable where you won't be disturbed.
- 'Make yourself tall': imagine there is a piece of string attached to the top your head and it is gently pulling your head upwards if you are sitting or away from your shoulders if you are lying down – try and let your body lengthen.
- Think about how your body feels; make sure your shoulders are not hunched up but are low towards your hips, and that your muscles are relaxed rather than tense.
- Now concentrate on your breathing; focus on your breath going in and out, concentrate on how it feels when your lungs fill up with air making your chest expand, then on how it feels when you exhale; do this five times.
- Now make your breathing deeper; breathe in slowly through

your nose for the count of five, filling your lungs more than you were before, and then out slowly through your mouth for the count of five; do this ten times ensuring you are only thinking about your breathing.

- Then slowly get up and notice how much more relaxed and calm you feel than you did before.

Progressive muscle relaxation is a great technique to help release tension in your muscles and body, and can work particularly well at bedtime or before meditation. It involves focusing on each muscle in the body and in turn tensing and then relaxing it to notice the contrasting feeling. This enables a feeling of deep muscle relaxation.

I know senior executives who use these techniques before important meetings, or who travel a lot and use the opportunity of being on the plane to meditate. I always make time for some calm deep breathing before a job interview.

There are plenty of books and websites giving you guidance on relaxation, meditation and mindfulness, there are specific classes you can attend and there are also very good apps that allow you to access instructions and exercises easily at times that suit you. Headspace (www.headspace.com) has some very good apps.

SLEEP, SLEEP AND MORE SLEEP

You can't underestimate the importance of sleep. Despite what people say they may be able to survive on, getting seven or eight hours of sleep per night has been shown to improve not only our energy levels and how we feel, but our mental functioning and our long-term health. Given this, why do so many of us regularly get less sleep than we really need?

Winding down with a regular routine during the evening is important for getting a good night's sleep. Not eating or exercising too near to your bedtime, having a relaxing bath or listening to some calming music before you go to bed and having a consistent time that you go to sleep all help. But even when doing this, it is not uncommon to find it difficult to switch off at night, or to find yourself waking early and not being able to get back to sleep.

This is usually because you have too much going round in your head to switch off and drop off. Using some of the relaxation and breathing techniques we've looked at will certainly help with this. A good technique is to write down everything in your head. This means you don't worry about remembering it, and it actively 'parks' the information until the morning. Keep a pen and paper by your bed, or if you're never more than an arm's length away from your smartphone just send yourself an email. Then try to keep your head clear. This is where being practised at meditation can really help as you will learn the skill of keeping your mind clear and calm. If, however, you are like me and haven't quite managed to crack that just yet, you can try distracting yourself so that those thoughts don't pop back into your head.

For some, reading a good book for a short period is enough to clear their head and get sleepy. I am always jealous of those people who can read at bedtime and drop off with the book still in their hands. How can anyone go to sleep that easily? It's not something that comes easily to me. If I'm reading a good book it makes my mind active and if my mind's active I can't sleep. Unfortunately, I have to do something that bores me. I read a really boring book (though unsurprisingly it's difficult to motivate myself to do that), or what I find works well is playing a bit of *FreeCell* on my phone. This gets boring very quickly and then with a clear mind I can drop right off to sleep!

A colleague once told me about a technique that someone shared with her to use if you wake up in the middle of the night and can't get back to sleep. You go through the alphabet thinking of five boy's names and five girl's names for each letter. For example, Adrian, Alan, Albert, Archie, Andrew and Anna, Alice, Anita, Amanda, Alyssa, then go on to the letter B. I find this works for me – again, I get so bored I just drop off. The colleague telling me said it doesn't work for her at all. When she gets to a letter where she can't think of five names she gets really irritated and wound up, which clearly wouldn't help anyone go to sleep.

Find out what works for you.

A WORD ON BURN-OUT

I used not to understand burn-out until it happened to me – fortunately not in a work context but in my short-lived sporting career as a slalom canoeist. I didn't recognize it as burn-out at the time, I just thought that I'd decided I didn't want to be a canoeist any more. I literally went from training 12 times a week and competing almost every weekend in the race season to not canoeing at all, not even recreationally. How could I have just completely stopped something that had been such an integral and important part of my life for so long? Something I loved so much and was driven to do purely from within?

The reality is that I'd had enough. I'd had enough because my approach to canoeing was not sustainable. I was so intense about it and focused my whole life on it so much that I became exhausted by it and lost my interest and motivation. I hadn't kept up any other sports that I had also enjoyed like tennis or netball, and it was so much about the winning that I perhaps lost the pure joy of white- water canoeing that got me hooked in the first place. Of course, it's possible that I only achieved what I did because of my intense focus, and that perhaps I couldn't have done it any other way. Luckily for me, the burn-out did not have significant consequences.

I decided to do something completely different; that's when I joined a samba band and had an amazing time playing fantastic gigs with great people. Exactly the change I needed.

In the workplace, though, situations that lead to burn-out can have much more serious consequences. Chronic stress, nervous break-downs, anxiety and all the negative health implications that come with these conditions can lead to burn-out. When you burn out it is common to lose interest and motivation, to find it hard to concentrate and, in extreme cases, to find it difficult to function normally.

This is why finding your sustainable way of working is so important. Finding your Work–Life Symbiosis – the way of living your life where everything contributes positively to everything else. You get energy from what you do, not drained or dragged down. If you feel constantly stressed at work, anxious, unhappy, overly tired or are working relentlessly long hours, it is not sustainable. You are at risk of burning out.

MAKING A COMMITMENT

Reading through tips and suggestions is one thing, but if you are going to actually make any change in your life, you need to be committed to and focused on what you will actually do differently. Start right now. Use this action-planning template to summarize the key actions you want to take going forward to enable yourself to be the best you can be – to be (absolutely) fabulous!

Action plan to enable me to be (*absolutely*) fabulous

THE ENVIRONMENT MOST ENABLING ME TO BE IN THE ZONE Is:

FACTORS IN MY CONTROL/INFLUENCE THAT IMPACT THIS ARE:

THE ACTIONS I WILL TAKE AS A RESULT ARE:

FACTORS OUTSIDE MY CONTROL THAT IMPACT THIS ARE:

THE POSITIVE SPIN ON THIS Is:

NOW THAT I KNOW MY CIRCADIAN RHYTHM I WILL:

TO BE MORE ACTIVE I WILL:

TO MAINTAIN CONCENTRATION MORE EFFECTIVELY I WILL:

TO DEVELOP A MORE POSITIVE MINDSET I WILL:

TO BE MORE MINDFUL I WILL:

TO GET MORE SLEEP I WILL:

CHAPTER

4

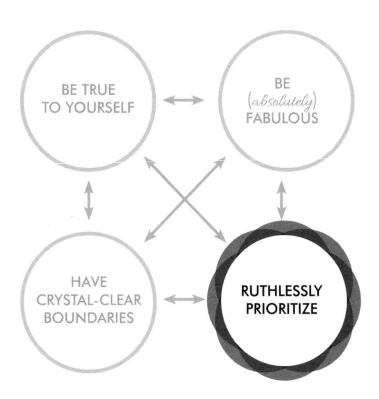

RUTHLESSLY PRIORITIZE

TAKING MATTERS INTO YOUR OWN HANDS

Obvious though it may seem, the need to prioritize 'ruthlessly' in work and life is not as easy as it sounds.

People often talk about how important it is to make choices and priority calls when you work part-time. They also say that you have to be extra efficient and effective. When I look at how many people in full-time roles work long hours, regularly into the evenings and at the weekends, I don't think it's an issue only for part-time employees. This is a challenge for everyone.

> BASICALLY WE ALL HAVE TOO MUCH TO DO AND IT'S HARD TO SAY NO.

Jobs are getting bigger. Organizations are often downsizing and restructuring. It's a regular occurrence for roles to be removed or two or more roles to be merged into one. But once this happens, organizations are often not good at taking work out and stopping things. Jobs left after organization changes need to be manageable and focused on the most critical and important responsibilities from the roles merged. This is difficult to achieve though so, instead, they are often just all the work that was there before, but now being done by only one person.

I have had many conversations with business leaders and managers in different organizations about roles in their teams and whether or not they could be done on a part-time basis.

The answer is usually "no". The manager is often so stretched in terms of their own workload and deliverables that they are unable to have the necessary creative thinking and foresight about this. They find it difficult to evolve their own vision of how each role could be done in a different way. They feel that everything is critical; there's too much work already for one full-time person (likely true) and there is nothing that could be stopped. However, people do tend to open their eyes and minds a little when I challenge them. And my challenge is this:

YOU SAY EVERY SINGLE THING HAS TO BE DONE AND COULDN'T POSSIBLY BE CHANGED. BUT NEXT MONTH, THE LEADERSHIP TEAM MAY WELL ANNOUNCE A RESTRUCTURE, OR A CUT-BACK. WHEN THIS HAPPENS THE VERY SAME MANAGERS WHO SAY NOTHING CAN BE CHANGED ARE TOLD, IN NO UNCERTAIN TERMS, THAT THEY NEED TO DECREASE THEIR TEAM FROM TWELVE TO EIGHT PEOPLE. THIS CAUSES ANGER AND FRUSTRATION AND MUCH TALK OF HOW IT CAN'T BE DONE. BUT IN THE END, OF COURSE, IT IS DONE. AND IRONICALLY THOSE ROLES THAT THE MANAGERS CLAIMED COULDN'T POSSIBLY BE DONE IN FOUR DAYS (INSTEAD OF FIVE) NOW NO LONGER EXIST AT ALL. NOT AT ALL. ZERO DAYS PER WEEK. YET, SOMEHOW, THE ORGANIZATION IS STILL FUNCTIONING AND, IN FACT, IS OFTEN IN BETTER SHAPE THAN IT WAS BEFORE BECAUSE IT HAS BEEN FORCED TO FIND WAYS TO BE MORE EFFICIENT AND EFFECTIVE.

So when someone says to me it's impossible to decrease the size of a role, I say to them, in a slightly more diplomatic way than this perhaps "Is it **really** not possible to find a way to manage the workload over a shorter period of time or is it that you aren't yet able to see how you could find a way to do it?"

Not all managers, or employees for that matter, are unskilled at prioritizing. Actually, all the really successful leaders I know are incredibly skilled at making tough choices, prioritizing and saying "no". In fact, they don't just prioritize,

they ruthlessly prioritize.

If we want to achieve Work–Life Symbiosis, this is a skill that we need to master both inside and outside work. Your workload, understandably, has a significant impact on how manageable your role is and how easy or not it is to work in a sustainable way. Given that most organizations and managers are still on a journey, in terms of being skilled at this and in designing appropriately sized jobs, we all need to take responsibility for doing this ourselves.

THE SWIMSUIT APPROACH

The thing about making priority choices is that we have to accept that some things won't get done. And we have to deal with that. There are only so many hours not just in the day, but in the working day. We have to embrace the concept that as long as we make the right priority choices, and get **the most important** things done, then the other things can wait, or be done by someone else, or in a different way, or, shock horror, not be done at all.

I'm not saying it's easy and clearly there will be some management of expectations necessary, but this is the simple truth of the matter.

A number of years ago, I had a lovely holiday in Portugal with my partner and four friends. On one of the days, we visited a water park (it was quite a few years ago but we were adults). We had a wonderful day full of relaxing, sunbathing and playing on the water slides. One of the slides was designed to be super-fast. It didn't go round any corners and was completely open. It had five shoots all alongside each other that basically just went down, over some bumps on the way, from the top to the bottom, very fast.

It was a popular one with the kids, and because it was open and in a straight line was a great one to watch people riding. As a result, the bottom of the slide was packed with spectators – parents taking photos and videos as their children flew down the slide screaming with joy. My mates and I thought this looked like great fun. Now, I'm not silly, I was aware that I was wearing a bikini. I realized the risk of my bikini top being pulled down and all the spectators getting an eye-full of more than they were expecting. But I had identified the risk, and was well prepared to mitigate it.

As I set off down the slide I had both my hands clasped tightly over my bikini top in the appropriate places to maintain my dignity, while having fun. Or so I thought. You see, I hadn't fully identified the risks. My bikini top stayed up, no problem. My bottoms, on the other hand, came right down. I mean right down. The spectators certainly got more than they bargained for. I had made the **wrong priority choice**. Quite honestly, if given the choice of saving my bikini bottoms or my bikini top, I would say what's the big deal about showing a bit of boob? I mean really, people sunbathe topless all the time, it's not that much of a big deal. If I'd thought this through properly, I would certainly not have chosen to hang on to the top half.

So I made what felt at the time like a pretty catastrophic job of prioritizing. Not only that, but what an example of bad planning – I mean, really, who goes to a water park with the intention of going on the slides wearing a bikini? Had I have done a better job of planning in advance, of fully identifying and considering all the risks, I could have made a decision that completely mitigated them both. I would, of course, have worn a swimsuit. Failing to prepare is preparing to fail.

Challenge yourself to ensure that you've fully understood **all** the risks associated with a particular decision or situation. Challenge yourself to find your own 'swimsuit approach' – mitigating all risks through good planning! If this isn't possible, make your priority decisions with your eyes wide open, understanding and accepting the implications.

IS IT URGENT OR IMPORTANT?

Dwight Eisenhower was the 34th president of the US, commander of the allied forces in Europe in World War II and a skilled organizer. He famously said: "What is important is seldom urgent and what is urgent is seldom important". A wise man indeed. From his philosophy came the renowned Urgent/Important Matrix, which Stephen Covey included in his book *7 Habits of Highly Effective People*, and which helps to identify where we should focus our time and attention, and can be used both inside and outside work.

Important tasks are things that contribute towards our long-term goals, strategy or values.

Urgent tasks are things that need immediate attention.

This approach forces us to consider what we are spending our time and energy on. It may sound silly; 'of course it's important otherwise I wouldn't be doing it!' But it's good to stop and reflect. It is common for people to do things or do them in a particular way, just because that's what's always been done, or indeed sometimes because that's what they like to do. Of course we don't like to think that things we spend time on are not important. Sometimes it's difficult not to wrap the value of what we are doing at work with our own personal value and self-worth. But you have to remember:

YOU ARE NOT YOUR WORK.

YOU ARE MUCH MORE THAN THAT.

You could be the most amazing, valued, productive, smart person in the world, but be working on something unimportant. It wouldn't make you any less valuable it would just make you poor at prioritizing, or possibly so efficient that you've already done all the important things.

There's also relativity. A task might seem important until compared to something else. It's important to have lunch. If you're at the airport, though, and it's the last call for your flight I think you'll decide to skip lunch in order to catch the plane.

Most people spend most of their time dealing with urgent tasks. When we do this we are being reactive and are responding to the demands around us rather than focusing on the things that will make a marked difference to what we actually want to achieve in the longer term. We get dragged into thinking that the urgent things are also important but they often are not. We are bombarded with so many things that if we only deal with the urgent things, which are usually short-term, we will never find the time to focus on the longer-term things.

Of course sometimes the urgent things do just need to be dealt with. When the 'shit is put on the fan', as my Brazilian mother-in-law would say (what she means to say is 'when the shit hits the fan'), we must give it our attention.

But we need to be conscious of what we are focusing on and why. Important tasks can sometimes be urgent, but often are not. This means dealing with important tasks tends to be more planned and proactive.

Eisenhower's Urgent/Important Matrix

	URGENT	NOT URGENT
IMPORTANT	**URGENT IMPORTANT** 'Critical' Examples: crisis situations, critical deadlines, key requests from important stakeholders, problem-solving	**NOT URGENT IMPORTANT** 'Important goals' Examples: longer-term financial objectives, delivering on a strategy, health and wellbeing, fitness, relationships, planning, personal growth and development
NOT IMPORTANT	**URGENT NOT IMPORTANT** 'Interruptions' Examples: people demanding responses, some meetings, responding to requests from others, some phone calls	**NOT URGENT NOT IMPORTANT** 'Distractions' Examples: anything that wastes time, surfing the internet, Facebook, Twitter, playing games, procrastinating, idle chat

On the face of it, it may seem that we should focus on those tasks that are both 'important and urgent'. However, this is not the case. The most crucial quadrant, and where we should invest most of our time and energy, is 'important but not urgent'. These are our long-term goals and objectives – the things that are most important and critical to us, whether we are thinking about inside or outside work. Unfortunately, these are the things that are most likely to be pushed aside as we deal with the general urgency of our lives and indulge, often subconsciously, in the multitude of distractions in modern life. Being clear on your Lifeboard will help inform you what should sit in your 'important but not urgent' quadrant.

You may be wondering how to use this tool in relation to work and home. This is an individual choice and depends on the situation you find yourself in. If currently you feel comfortable with how you manage your time and energy outside work, but work is a struggle, then focus on work. If, on the other hand, you have work under control, but it's outside work that you want to make changes, focus on home. If, as many people do, you feel that both could do with a bit of a tweak, then you can focus on both.

As mentioned in chapter 1, the propensity to approach home and work as integrated or not is very much a personal choice and often one that people feel very strongly about; like Marmite, if you will (Marmite is a British spread with a strong taste that, according to the marketing message, people tend to either love or hate). For some people, it works well to grab a few spare minutes at work, during a break from looking at the computer screen, to make those phone calls to the doctors, the insurance company and the bank. Others want to compartmentalize work and home and deal with each separately.

If you prefer the latter, I would suggest that you plot one matrix covering work tasks to review where you should be spending your time and how you should be prioritizing, and a separate one for home. If you prefer the former, and feel that all tasks in your life whether they are home or work need to be balanced against one another, then use one integrated matrix covering both.

PLOTTING YOUR OWN URGENT/ IMPORTANT MATRIX
Follow these four steps to plot your matrix:

1) Choose whether you are focusing on home, work or both.
2) Capture, on the matrix template below, all the things you spend your time on currently and allocate them to the appropriate quadrant. Keep in mind that, for things to be considered 'important', they should contribute to longer-terms goals or objectives. For example, in a work context, these could be things that directly relate to your core job: annual

targets, teaching lessons, seeing patients, clients or customers, department goals, objectives or vision, or company strategy and targets.

3) Consider and capture all the things that are important that you **don't** currently spend time on. For example, that piece of work on a team vision or revising a lesson plan or piece of work you've been meaning to do, or investing in your personal development.

4) Consider and capture anything urgent that you aren't spending time on.

Use these prompting questions when thinking about a task or piece of work to challenge yourself about which box it should sit in. Try to be both ruthless and honest. There may be things that you enjoy spending your time on that if you really search your soul you will have to admit aren't actually important.

PROMPTING QUESTIONS

For each task or piece of work, ask yourself:

- Is it part of my core job and what I am expected to do on a day-to-day or week-to-week basis?
- Does it contribute to my agreed annual objectives or what I want to achieve this year, or in the longer term?
- Is it about my personal development?
- Is it in line with the department or company strategy or approach, or my personal life strategy?
- Does it support someone else's development or support them personally?
- Is it a favour or gesture of goodwill to someone, using an appropriate amount of my time and energy?
- Is it good for my health, wellbeing or fitness?

If the answer to **all** these questions is "no", then I would suggest ideally you should <u>not do it</u> **at all**. In this case, consider the following questions:

- Does it HAVE to be done and if so, why? Remember to be ruthless.
- What will happen if it isn't done and can this be mitigated?
- Can it be postponed?
- Can it be done by someone else? If so, by whom?
- Who do I need to review or discuss this with?

Plot your own Urgent/Important Matrix:

	URGENT	NOT URGENT
IMPORTANT	URGENT IMPORTANT	NOT URGENT IMPORTANT
NOT IMPORTANT	URGENT NOT IMPORTANT	NOT URGENT NOT IMPORTANT

If you are finding it difficult to complete the matrix, or to sense-check it, it's a good idea to spend a few days writing down exactly what you do. Sometimes what we think we spend our time on and what we actually spend our time on are not the same but it's difficult to identify this unless we actually capture what we do. There are some good time management apps you can use for this, such as

'Schedule Planner' from Digi117, where you can capture exactly how you spent the time in your day. With this app, you can also contrast this with how you intended to spend your time. Or you can use a simple pen and paper, and just write down in blocks of 30 minutes or so what you are doing.

Once you've filled in your matrix, look at what it is telling you. Where are you spending your time? Is it where you want to be spending your time? Why are you spending your time there?

Consider what's in your 'important but not urgent' quadrant. Are you spending enough time on these things to make the amount of progress with which you are happy? What is stopping you spending more time here? What can you do about this? Spending time in this quadrant should be your utmost priority because these are the things that actually contribute to what's on your Lifeboard or are the essence of your job. Schedule time to do these tasks – block sections of your diary so that other meetings can't crop up, and commit to yourself not to cancel at the last minute in favour of something that feels more urgent. Arranging meetings or time to work on these areas with other people can help because this creates a commitment that you are more likely to stick to.

Consider what's in your 'important and urgent' quadrant. What sort of things are they? Is there anything proactive you can do to reduce the number of times things come up here? Is there any way you could deal more efficiently or quickly with these things? For example, if key deadlines keep creeping up and becoming urgent, could you plan ahead better to keep projects or tasks on track without becoming urgent? If you keep having to invest time in getting the car fixed or trying to fix your bicycle, might it be time to buy a new one?

Consider what's in your 'urgent and not important' quadrant. A lot of time gets spent here, with people mistakenly thinking they are spending time on things that are both urgent and important.

These tasks are often helping other people and so can feel important, but you have to keep in mind to whom they are important. You should help and support others, and sometimes we need to do this whether it suits us or not. But it can be easy to put too much time and energy into things that are important to others to the detriment of focusing on what is important to you. You need to strike the right balance. Help others, yes, but

> ENSURE THAT YOUR LIFE, TIME AND ENERGY CHOICES ARE DEFINED BY WHAT'S IMPORTANT TO YOU, NOT TO SOMEONE ELSE.

Of course, what is important to you might be making others in your life happy. That's your choice.

Consider whether anything in this box can be done by anyone else, or whether in fact the response to the request simply has to be "no". Saying "no" is usually not easy, but I have some tips that I will come on to that will help.

Consider what's in your 'not urgent and not important' quadrant. Be honest here. Sometimes it's difficult to admit to ourselves or even genuinely remember how much time we spend procrastinating. I find it's a bit like really knowing what you eat. When you think about what you ate during the day you remember the main meals but unless you actually pay conscious attention, or write down what you eat through the day, it's easy to forget the extras. The biscuit you had with your coffee, the third slice of toast at breakfast, the couple of chocolates you had with your tea, or the crisps your friend kindly shared with you.

Unless you've planned time in to read the news, check Twitter or Snapchat with your friends, don't do it! A friend of mine recently posted the following as her Facebook status:

THAT'S IT, I AM LEAVING SOCIAL MEDIA. I HAVE REALIZED I WASTE MY LIFE – I JUST LOOKED AT THE ARTICLE '13 POTATOES THAT LOOK LIKE CHANNING TATUM'!

I think that says it all. So be strong – make more time to focus on the important things.

To decrease the chance of being distracted from what you want to focus on, try setting a timer. Work solidly for a period of time, when the timer goes off reward yourself with a little break, a cup of tea or coffee, a nice cheese scone perhaps, a change of task, or the pure and simple satisfaction of having concentrated so well.

Completing your own Urgent/Important Matrix will have shed light on choices you can make to manage your time and focus in a different way. You may have realized that some of what you are spending time on is not what you should be spending time on. The tricky part is whether those around you will agree with this or not.

If you think there are people who will not agree with your perspective on the changes you want to make, for example, your boss, your colleagues, or perhaps friends or family, it is important to address this. In the workplace, you should discuss and gain agreement about what you will and will not do. Outside work, you will need to ensure that your expectations are aligned with those of others. This will involve explaining the changes you want to make and the rationale behind them. In some cases, it may turn out that there are factors of which you were unaware that prevent you from making these changes. In other instances, it may be necessary for you to make an alternative suggestion about how things that you will no longer do can be managed in a different way. We can explore this in more detail in the following chapter, where I will talk about managing difficult conversations.

Take time to reflect on what you have learnt from the urgent/ important exercise and note down your thoughts:

WHAT DOES MY MATRIX TELL ME?

WHERE AM I SPENDING MOST OF MY TIME AND WHY?

WHERE DO I WANT TO SPEND MY TIME?

WHAT CAN I DO TO MAKE THIS HAPPEN?

WHO DO I NEED TO DISCUSS THIS WITH AND WHOSE BUY-IN DO I NEED?

WHAT IF THERE ARE JUST TOO MANY IMPORTANT THINGS?

It is possible that one of your reflections having used the Urgent/ Important Matrix is that there are just too many important things to have time for. That even with the prioritization that has come from reviewing your time and energy management in this way, there are just not enough hours in the day to do all the things that you really feel are important.

This is where **ruthless prioritization** really comes into its own.
To start with, we have to be realistic about how much time we have available, and how long it takes us to do things. People constantly underestimate the amount of time things take, planning an unrealistic number of objectives or activities in a set amount of time. This leads to the disappointment of not achieving what you set out to do, and spending more time on things than you allowed for. This has the knock-on effect that the rest of your day is running late and likely more stressful than it should have been or needs to be. The simple truth is that if there is too much to get done in any set amount of time, you have to decide what you will do and what you will not do. To do this effectively, you need to understand and accept the risks and consequences of your decisions. Remember the swimsuit approach?

WHAT WILL HAPPEN IF YOU DON'T DO IT?

Sometimes we feel like things HAVE to be done. But what's really the worst-case scenario if they aren't? Often, it isn't all that bad in the end.

I used to think I was ultra-organized and efficient by keeping track of when I had to renew the annual parking permit for my car to allow me to park on our street. I kept a note in my diary, and in plenty of time I would go on line, find the form, download the form, print the form, fill in all the details and send it off for my new permit. After a couple of years (yes, it took me that long), I realized that if I just did nothing, took no action at all, then the council would send me a letter telling it was time to renew the permit. It would include a pre-completed form with all my details that I only needed to sign and return. Less effort on my part and one less thing for which I had to feel responsible.

> SOMETIMES WE NEED TO LET GO,
> AND TRUST THAT SOMEONE ELSE WILL DO IT.

This applies at work too. Make sure that there's a clear purpose or output for the things you spend your time on. If you're doing something for someone else, you may need to challenge them to ensure they know what the benefit of doing the task is, and possibly doing it in that particular way.

WHY IS IT SO HARD TO SAY NO?

Most of us find it difficult to say no when someone asks us to do something that we don't want, or don't have time, to do. Why is that? Do we feel guilty? Is it a desire to please others? Is it that we feel awkward? Whatever the reason, most of us would benefit from being better at it. Here are some tips that might help:

- Be nice. Just because you are turning down the request doesn't mean you can't be terribly polite about it.
- Acknowledge that they've asked you to do it – this is usually a compliment as you're the person with the right skills and they trust you will deliver.
- If you feel you aren't able to say no straight away, or you want to reflect on the request, simply ask for some time. Tell them you need to think it through and will let them know later.
- If you are able to make the decision there and then be firm and

clear. Try not to "um" or "err", just simply say that you aren't able to do what they ask.

- Only offer an explanation if it's necessary. Don't feel like you have to make excuses. In a lot of situations it's perfectly acceptable to just say no. If you do think an explanation is necessary, keep it clear, factual and unapologetic.
- If you have said no, don't back down when pressured. This will make saying no the next time even harder. Be resolute in your decision.
- If you feel guilty, it's fine to let them know that you would really like to be able to say yes, but alas, you can't.
- Make sure it's not personal – you're saying no about the task, not saying no to the person asking, and ensure they understand this.
- If there are things that could be done or changed that would enable you to say yes, explain them and see if they are possible.
- Acknowledge that they may be disappointed or that this may put them in a difficult position (but don't back down).
- If possible, make an alternative suggestion about how the work or task can be managed in a different way.
- Understand the implications of saying no. It may mean you miss out on something or the person who asked is irritated. These things need to be accepted as unfortunate consequences of the right decision.

If you are expecting someone to ask you to do something that you want to say no to, plan in advance what you will say. It's much easier to say something that feels difficult if you have worked out in advance a couple of clear and simple sentences that get your message across.

Be mindful though. If you are in a situation where you feel you are consistently being asked to do things that you don't have time for or you don't think you should be doing, then it is important to raise this with the individual asking you. The two of you clearly have misaligned expectations and this should be explored.

PERSONAL EFFECTIVENESS REALLY IS PERSONAL

It sounds obvious but I can't emphasize enough that what works for me probably won't work for you and vice versa. We all need to find our own way of being efficient and effective, and our own way of making decisions.

A friend of mine has a dog she called 'Tay'. He was so named after the river Tay because of personal connections to both Dundee, through which the river Tay runs, and the river itself from having regularly crossed it as a student. She also liked the fact that it was a name that no other dog was likely to have and is short and snappy to call in the park. The perfect choice, I believe.

If I were to follow this logic, however, by naming a dog after the waterway to which I felt most connected, it would have to be called 'Basingstoke Canal'. It was on the Basingstoke canal that I first learnt to canoe and spent many hours training. A name that no other dog will be called, granted, but not all that snappy to call in the park, or at any time in fact. Not the perfect choice in my case.

It's easy to get wrapped up in what others do and the approach they take. Even without realizing we are doing it, we often go about things in a particular way because that's how it's always been done. It's important to stop, think, and work out the right approach for you at that point, in that situation. It will change and evolve depending on the context or challenge. Try to keep an open mind – the right approach might be one that hasn't been taken before.

Dame Shirley Stephanie, a British business woman and philanthropist, in her 2012 book *Let it Go – The Memories of Dame Stephanie Shirley*, gives a fascinating insight into how forward-thinking it's possible to be if you are not constrained by 'the norm'. In 1962, she set up her own company called Freelance Programmers, because she was frustrated by the prejudice and sexism she experienced in the workplace. The company specifically focused on offering employment to highly intelligent and talented female computer programmers who had dropped out, or been pushed out, of the traditional male-dominated workforce, often as a result of having children.

The working practices Dame Stephanie put in place made complete sense to her – these women worked from home, while looking after their children, on a project basis, in the hours that suited them and were measured only on their outputs, not their inputs. She wasn't aware of, and therefore wasn't influenced by, the working practices at the time, which were focused very much on inputs and close monitoring and control of what employees did. Most people were still clocking in and out at the time. What she did would be still be considered pretty revolutionary now, and certainly best practice in terms of approach to flexible and agile working, let alone in the 1960s. She just did what made sense to her and met the needs of her business, without the pressure of knowing what everyone else was doing and how different this was.

USING YOUR COMMUTE

If you possibly can, avoid commuting. It's a killer – it sucks time and is exhausting; live near work, work near home or, better still, from home. If you have to commute, though, and I realize most of us do, make the most of the time. What making the most of it looks like is, of course, your choice, but make a choice. We've already considered using commuting time to exercise, but you see plenty of other examples on the train, the bus or the tube: power napping, putting on make-up, reading a book or newspaper, playing games, managing emails. I saw a bloke doing pull-ups from the overhead hand rails on the tube once!

I used to have a 30-minute train journey to work in the morning and the evening. I used the time to keep on top of my work emails. This was working time – I didn't do it on top of a long working day in the office, this I counted as part of my working day, and a very efficient use of time it was too. Without that opportunity I would basically have had no chance whatsoever of staying even vaguely in control of my emails. I would also sometimes use the time on the train to work to prepare for a meeting that morning.

I realize not everyone has this flexibility, but if you give it some serious thought, there may be more opportunity than you imagine, to use your commuting time in a way that works for you.

From the station to the office was either a five-minute shuttle bus journey, which I took if I had an early meeting, or a 20-minute walk. I would try to walk because, of course, it's good for you (remember the 20 minutes a day of moderate activity?), but also it was excellent time to catch up on voicemails or phone calls I needed to make. I could drive to work instead and I would do this when I had a speech or presentation coming up. I would use the time in the car to practise out loud what I was planning to say. I found this made a significant difference to the quality of my performance.

DO WHAT WORKS FOR YOU

Sometimes, you have a piece of work that you just can't seem to move forward. Maybe you need thinking time that you never seem to be able to get. In this situation, I go for a long run. But you could take a walk, be on a journey, or be pushing a sleeping baby around in a buggy. I find this is an excellent example of multi-tasking! I am getting exercise while having completely undisturbed thinking time about something I need to move forward. On these runs, I always manage to make significant progress on my work. The things we can't seem to move forward are never insurmountable, they usually just need mental attention. I come through the door after the run full of ideas and thoughts and immediately start making notes to capture it all. I have always made a great deal more progress than I would have done sitting at my desk.

A global vice-president who used to be my boss always managed her emails on a Sunday. I challenged her once and said I didn't think she was setting a good example to the team. That she should role-model not working in the evenings or at weekends because otherwise the team felt like they have to do that also. She pushed back and said very clearly that she absolutely did not expect me or the team to work long hours or at weekends. She expected us to deliver on our expectations but manage our time how we wanted to in order to achieve this. She also said that the way she wanted to manage her time to achieve this was to check her emails on a Sunday. This was her choice.

She wanted to do this so that when she came into work on Monday morning she knew that she wouldn't be blind-sided by the CEO asking her about something that had come through over the weekend of which she wasn't aware. She pointed out that, just as she should let me work in a way that suited me, I needed to let her work in a way that suited her. She made it clear that she didn't expect me to work at weekends, so if I felt pressure to do so because she did, that was my baggage, not hers.

I thought this was an excellent point.

I have also seen brilliant examples of individuals at director level managing their day in a way that worked for them. For example, working until 3pm, then picking up children from school and spending time with them, and doing another couple of hours work in the evening. I've seen this work successfully in teams where the culture was not to work in this way at all. But a talented, driven individual, clear on what would and would not work for her, came in and got on with it. She delivered on everything, but just managed it in her own way, and no one could argue. I realize this will not be possible everywhere, but it does show it is possible somewhere.

Here are some ideas to consider to help you make your effectiveness more personal:

- Schedule specific time for important tasks or work.
- Block out periods of time in your calendar to ensure you don't end up in back-to-back meetings, and you have some breathing space in which to do the urgent things that come up, whether they are important or not.
- Turn your phone off and close your emails and communicator when you want to work on something without being disturbed.
- Turn off your phone and email when you don't want to work at all.
- Plan more time than you think you will need – things always take longer than we expect.
- Focus on one thing at a time. Multi-tasking is often not all that efficient. Things tends to take longer and be of lower quality when we are concentrating on multiple things at once.
- Know how good 'good enough' is. To the perfectionists out there, this may sound both impossible and silly. But, actually, it's really important. Spend the necessary time on something to make it good enough. Then stop and move on to one of the other things you need to get done. Be pragmatic.
- Focus on outputs not inputs.
- Rank tasks in priority order and do the most important ones first.

MAKING A COMMITMENT

Having reviewed different approaches to managing time and prioritizing, and having heard examples of actions other people take, it's time to consider what you will do differently. Use the action-planning template over the page to summarize the key actions you want to take going forward to ruthlessly prioritize.

Action plan to enable you to prioritize ruthlessly

THE ACTIONS I WILL TAKE IN LIGHT OF MY URGENT/
IMPORTANT MATRIX ARE:

I WILL SAY "NO" MORE BY:

I WILL USE MY COMMUTING
TIME FOR:

THE THINGS I WILL STOP
DOING ARE:

THE ACTIONS I WILL TAKE TO
MAKE MYSELF MORE 'PERSONALLY'
EFFECTIVE ARE:

THE ACTIONS I WILL TAKE TO MAKE TOUGHER PRIORITY CHOICES ARE:

I WILL MANAGE THE RELEVANT INDIVIDUALS BY:

HAVE CRYSTAL-CLEAR BOUNDARIES

CHAPTER

5

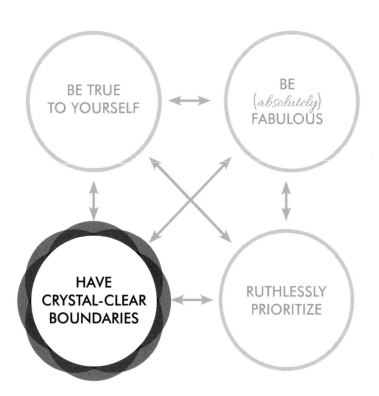

BE TRUE
TO YOURSELF

BE
(absolutely)
FABULOUS

HAVE
CRYSTAL-CLEAR
BOUNDARIES

RUTHLESSLY
PRIORITIZE

HAVE CRYSTAL-CLEAR BOUNDARIES

DEFINING YOUR BOUNDARIES

In order to manage your boundaries, you need to be crystal-clear what they are.

How can your expectations be met if you, and other people for that matter, don't know what those expectations are? I know people who are unhappy with the amount of time they spend working, and the frequency with which this is either late into the evening or at the weekend. But when I ask them how many evenings or weekends they are happy to work, or how many of their children's bedtimes per week are they comfortable missing, they don't know the answer. They are clear their current situation is neither sustainable nor acceptable, but they are not clear on what it needs to look like instead. This makes it almost impossible to address.

As with most things I have discussed so far, your boundaries will be personal. They will likely depend on things such as what's most important to you, the stage of your life, your other commitments, how you feel about your role at the time, the demands of your job and the company culture.

ONE THING IS CLEAR, THOUGH - IT SHOULD BE YOU DEFINING YOUR BOUNDARIES; NOT SOMEONE ELSE.

As I have said, I love my job, I love my career and I have a very high need to achieve, in whatever I do. But I have never worked 'long' hours. There's just too much more to life. That has taken effort though and has always been a conscious choice.

I was once asked, in a job interview for a director-level role, what the worst thing about a job would be for me. Not exactly a textbook best-practice question, but alas, they often aren't. I thought about whether to offer some cheesy corporate answer but decided, as usual, to tell the truth. I told him that I love my job, and I always achieve what I need to, and more. I also love what I do outside work, for example, spending time with family and friends and playing sport, and that doing those things gives me energy to do a better job in work. So, the worst thing about a job for me would be if I were consistently and regularly expected to work long days or at the weekends. I explained that I realized that sometimes long hours were needed to get things done for a specific reason, and that I had no issue with that, but not always working long hours. This would not allow me to have the time or energy to do the other things I love and would grind me down. It would mean I wasn't at my best in or out of work.

His response started positively, saying that he totally understood, and that he put his family first. But then he torpedoed that part of his answer by proceeding to tell me that in order to avoid working at the weekends, so that he could spend time with his family, during the week he works 12-hour days in the office…

Right then, my kids are barely awake for much more than 12 hours a day. I felt I had been very clear about what was important to me in terms of having the time to focus on my family and things outside work. And although he said he agreed and understood this, his answer showed such a different interpretation of this concept that I felt we were on completely different wavelengths about what this meant to us. This did not feel workable.

The approach of working 12-hour weekdays in order to focus on the family at the weekend may work for him, but would certainly not work for me. It's not my idea of putting family first.

I pulled out of the application process for the role the next day.

There is a wise expression that says "you join a company but you leave a boss". This means that, when you choose to take a job at a new organization, it's based on what you know about that organization – the philosophy or mission, the opportunity it affords you, what they do, or the culture. When you choose to leave an organization it tends not to be about those things, but actually is more often about your line manager, how they manage you, what they are like and the relationship you have with them. In my experience, this is very true indeed.

One of my more brilliant managers over the years had a progressive attitude to ways of working. He believed in measuring outputs not inputs, as many people do, but he also passionately believed that people should not work an unrealistic and unsustainable number of hours per week. He believed this because he saw the value, benefit and importance of investing in things other than work. He also had a good business rationale. He pointed out, which I hadn't considered before, that if everyone was working flat out at absolute maximum capacity all the time, doing long hours and working weekends just to do their normal 'day job', not only is this unsustainable but the organization has no capacity left to 'flex upwards' when needed.

Invariably things happen – critical or even crisis situations that need to be dealt with. Projects have problems, people are off sick, customers complain, products have faults, or mergers or acquisitions take place. In these situations, additional work is needed. If everyone is already working flat out just to get the everyday work done there is no capacity to 'flex upwards' the amount of time and energy people are able to invest.

His pragmatic and absolutely sensible approach was that people's normal regular working patterns and habits need to be reasonable and sustainable. Then, when something out of the ordinary demands additional time and attention, people have the capacity to put more time and energy in for a short period of time to deal with this, without everything else having to be dropped.

There is, of course, the question of how or whether this should be compensated. Many organizations are explicit in their contract that although there might be core hours, employees are expected to work the number of hours necessary to get the job done. This works when a manager or supervisor has a positive attitude towards Work–Life Symbiosis and allows people to 'flex downwards' as well as 'flex upwards'. In some organizations, overtime is paid or time off 'in lieu' can be taken, where an employee is given time off work in addition to a normal holiday allowance to compensate for hours worked over and above what is contracted.

Make sure you understand the approach where you work, and make sure you are treated fairly. For example, if there is a time-off-in-lieu policy, track the additional hours you work and ensure that you actually take the additional time off.

YOUR BOUNDARIES STATEMENT

It's always best to write down your boundaries. It's much easier to stick to, and understand, something that's committed to paper, or these days 'to screen'. My boundaries have changed and evolved over the years as my life situation has changed, and this is to be expected.

They should reflect your current situation, reality and life goals and will likely be a bit different next year or the year after. Not everyone has flexibility in their working patterns, but as an example, in a previous role my boundaries statement looked like this:

MY WORK BOUNDARIES

- I work four days per week, between roughly the hours of 8.30am and 5.30pm, which includes working on my journey to and from work.
- I am actually in the office approximately three days per week between the hours of 9am and 4.45pm
- On one of my days in the office I go to the gym at lunchtime and then work for an hour that evening to compensate
- I work from home, on average, once per week

If you are in a role with less flexibility or autonomy, for example with set working patterns, specific start and finish times and no opportunity to get on with work tasks when you aren't in your place of work, then your boundaries will be different. They might be more focused on how much overtime you work, or the notice you get to work it, about your break times, the type of work you are expected to do, how the work is done and managed, or how your working hours or shift patterns are organized.

If you need more help shaping your thoughts around how to create the type of boundaries that work for you, the Center for Creative Leadership (www.ccl.org) has a useful tool called WorkLife Indicator, developed by the Center for Creative Leadership in combination with Ellen Kossek, PhD and author of *CEO of me* (published in 2007). The indicator is a self-assessment, found in the 'assessment tools & resources' section of the leadership development area of the website, which gives a feedback report covering areas such as the degree to which you combine or separate your work and family life; the degree to which you identify with and invest yourself in work and family life; and the degree to which you feel in control of how you manage your boundaries between your work and personal life.

Once you are ready to create your own boundaries statement, do the following:

- Revisit your Lifeboard and remind yourself what you identified as being most important to you in life.
- Think about the ideas you came up with to enable you to be (absolutely) fabulous, and how they may impact your boundaries.
- Review your actions relating to ruthlessly prioritizing and consider any impact this might have.
- Think about your personal situation and job context – the type of work that needs to be done and the different ways in which this might be achieved.
- Keep in mind your organization's policies in relation to ways of working, such as flexible, agile or home working, or how shifts are managed. Do not let this dictate your boundaries, though; it might be that you need to find somewhere else to work in order to live by the boundaries you want to have.

With this in mind, capture what you think you want your boundaries to be by writing your own boundaries statement.

MY BOUNDARIES:

....

....

....

....

....

As well as being clear on what your typical week looks like, it's important to have a view on what is not acceptable also. Again, in a previous role, that looked like this:

WHAT IS <u>NOT</u> ACCEPTABLE FOR ME

- **Ever** being late to collect my children from school or nursery for a work-related reason. If I can arrange for someone else to collect them at the last minute that is ok occasionally, but not having alternative arrangements in place and me being late (for example, nursery or school being shut and me not being there) is never ok for me.
- Very long work trips away from home (more than a week), unless in exceptional circumstances.
- Being expected to respond to my work phone at weekends or on non-work days, unless in exceptional circumstances.
- Frequently being expected, or having, to work in the evenings or at weekends, unless this is a deliberate pattern I have established – for example, to compensate for going to the gym during the day.

Consider this in your context, and in relation to your boundaries statement. Capture what would not be acceptable for you:

WHAT IS <u>NOT</u> ACCEPTABLE FOR ME:

....

....

....

....

....

....

....

....

....

....

....

....

When I first left university, I worked as a fitness instructor in a big health club. I enjoyed it very much and worked hard when I was there. I took on additional projects because I was motivated to, like designing and implementing a better system for managing cards with each of the member's fitness programmes on them. No one could say I wasn't committed or motivated. We worked shifts, and I was part-time, which seems ironic now because at the time I desperately wanted to work full-time but part-time was all that was available. Now it's the other way around: I want to work part-time but have found there are significantly fewer opportunities as a result.

Once a month, there were staff meetings. Attending these was not in our contracts, but we were expected to be there nonetheless, even if we weren't working that day. We were not paid for this time. It took me half an hour to drive to work and the meetings were an hour. So if I attended it would basically be the best part of half a day on a non-working day taken up by this and for nothing in return financially. I thought this was unreasonable and so raised it with the gym manager. She understood my point of view and, in fact, the reality of the case was that attendance of people not on shift was very poor indeed – most people just didn't turn up regardless, without actually discussing it with her.

She was not able to agree to pay people for attendance at these meetings. However, as a result of our discussion, she acknowledged that she understood why we felt it was an unreasonable expectation. Going forward, the approach she took was to ensure all employees not on shift knew they were welcome to attend if they so wished, but were not expected, and that an update of what was discussed would be circulated to everyone to ensure those who hadn't attended were kept in the loop. A good outcome I thought.

THE NEED FOR FLEXIBILITY

Life and work doesn't always pan out as we expect or hope. It's important to be open to this. In addition to being clear on boundaries and on what you feel are reasonable exceptions, it is also important to be flexible. Trying to be too rigid can be stressful for you and can be frustrating for employers and colleagues.

When I first started to work part-time, I wanted to work four days per week with Fridays off – who wouldn't want Fridays off? It wasn't just that it was the end of the week, though; it was the day my partner already had off looking after the children. The point was to spend a three-day weekend together as a family. So it wouldn't actually have met my need to have any other day off instead at that point. I was the HR director for the business and unfortunately the two-day monthly leadership team meeting, which I was not only expected but wanted to attend, was always on a Thursday and Friday.

Clearly, this posed an issue. It would have been unreasonable for me to expect this to be changed – these meetings are planned out a year in advance and everyone else's diaries are managed around them. It would certainly not be acceptable for me not to attend, and I wanted to attend – being part of the leadership team and therefore attending the meetings was a critical part of the role, and a part that I enjoyed.

My manager and I discussed the possibilities and he suggested that once a month I could swap the day that I didn't work. So, for example, I could work on the Friday but not work on the Monday that week. The point of having a day off though was to spend time with my family and on all other days my partner was at work and my children were in various childcare arrangements. So as nice as it would have been to have a day off all to myself, I couldn't really justify that. We agreed then that I would, instead, work and be paid for the additional day. This meant that instead of working and being paid for 80% of a full-time role (which would equate to four days per week) I would work and be paid for 84% of a full-time role (which equated to four days per week plus one additional day per month). This suited the business and me.

At other times in my career, I have simply worked four days per week. When the occasional ad hoc situation has come up when it's appropriate or needed for me to work on my non-work day we have addressed it on a case-by-case basis. Usually I will suggest how we deal with it, which would either be swapping my day off that week or taking an additional day of holiday to use at another time.

As long as you have a positive relationship with your manager or supervisor and a mindset of wanting to accommodate the needs of the business where possible, managing planned ad hoc changes can be simple. The type of flexibility I find harder to accommodate, and less reasonable to expect, is when it's last-minute.

I remember working with one colleague who to start with used to regularly forget that I didn't work on a Monday or that I had to leave work in time to pick up the children from nursery. We had a big joint project we were working on and often had to plan in time to spend together on it. He would suggest Mondays and I had to keep reminding him that I didn't work that day. It was also not unusual at the beginning for him to say, when we were in the middle of working on something complex: "I can stay as late as is needed tonight", implying that we could work together on it during the evening, which clearly I usually could not. Once I got so frustrated with this that I asked him "how exactly do you expect my two- and three-year-old children to get home from nursery tonight then? Walk home on their own?"

What I realized was that the people around you need to get used to a different way of working as well as you and your manager. Having colleagues working with different patterns or hours is generally not what people are used to, and it may not fit in with their way of working either. For many people, staying late in the evening may well be their approach to keeping on top of their workload when something comes up unexpectedly. It may be their preference to stay late in response to this to get it dealt with that evening rather than have it impact the rest of the week by needing to be dealt with the following day. It's important to understand each other's working preferences and be able to find ways to accommodate both approaches. We found ways to do this.

People use flexibility in different ways. I know a father who has a big role with a lot of responsibility in the City. When he is working on a deal he works very long hours and doesn't spend much time with his family. However, in between deals, he makes sure he spends time during the working day with them to compensate for this. It works well for them.

It is important to think through what a **reasonable level of flexibility** looks like for you and how you can manage this.

An example of this, based on my boundaries statement and what I have identified as not acceptable, is as follows:

ACCEPTABLE SOMETIMES	IN WHICH CIRCUMSTANCES?	HOW FREQUENTLY?	HOW CAN I PROACTIVELY AVOID THIS HAPPENING TOO OFTEN?
Working after the kids are in bed	During a particularly busy period or if I had a long gym session at lunchtime	Due to gym, weekly; due to busy period, on average a couple of times a month	Keep periods of time clear in your diary on a weekly basis, for example a two-hour slot, to give yourself flexibility to deal with unexpected urgent things. Prioritize when needed by delegating or putting on hold other work to give yourself time to deal with critical things. If this happens regularly, try allowing more time than you currently do to get work done so that it doesn't spill over the end of the working day.
Working at the weekend	Due to a business critical project/ piece of work	Quarterly on average	As suggested above. In addition, if you have a big critical piece of work, or are feeling overwhelmed by volume of work, look ahead at your diary for the next few weeks. Instead of cancelling your weekend, find some work to cancel. Identify meetings or commitments that can be cancelled or postponed, then identify meetings or events to which you can send someone in your place. This creates time and space for you to focus on what's critical and can give others a new opportunity.

ACCEPTABLE SOMETIMES	IN WHICH CIRCUMSTANCES?	HOW FREQUENTLY?	HOW CAN I PROACTIVELY AVOID THIS HAPPENING TOO OFTEN?
Missing putting the kids to bed due to work commitments	Important evening event/meeting that is key for me to attend	Two or three times per month on average	Prioritize only the events or meetings that are critical for you to attend. Give other people the opportunity to attend events or meetings on your behalf and share key outputs with you and a wider team afterwards. Seek out daytime events that meet your needs instead of evening ones.
Responding to work phone on non-work day	Due to a business critical project/ piece of work	Once per month on average	Empower and develop other people to be able to deal with things in your absence. Ensure your stakeholders know who they can contact when you are not working. If something or someone really could wait until you are back at work, let it/them wait. Make it clear upfront that unless it is an emergency, you do not expect to be contacted on your non-work day.

Consider the level of flexibility you find acceptable in the context of your boundaries statement, Lifeboard and role, and complete the following for yourself:

ACCEPTABLE SOMETIMES	IN WHICH CIRCUMSTANCES?	HOW FREQUENTLY?	HOW CAN I PROACTIVELY AVOID THIS HAPPENING TOO OFTEN?

YOUR BOUNDARIES ARE YOUR RESPONSIBILITY

Being clear on your boundaries is the first step. Then you need to live by them. The chances are, no one is going to protect your boundaries for you. That's your job. Of course ideally you would have a respectful and excellent manager who did notice and suggest that you go home after a certain time, but for most people this is unlikely to be the case. If we want to work in a different way, we need to make it work ourselves.

I saw an unfortunate example where a senior-level employee moved from working four days to three days per week. This was agreed on a trial basis. Unfortunately, she did not protect her boundaries at all, and neither did the business. She was asked consistently and regularly to work on her days off and she agreed to do this, because she could see that people were busy and under pressure. She kept an eye on her BlackBerry on her non-work days too. She was constantly aware of the pressures from the projects she was working on. As a result, she felt an expectation to do yet more work on her days off. She resented this situation because she was not being paid for this time, and because of the pattern that had been established couldn't see a way to change it. This continued for an extended period and in the end she was not able to sustain the situation. Sadly, it resulted in her having to take time off work to recover. The company now have a view that working three days per week at that level is not possible and will therefore not entertain the idea for anyone else. The truth of the matter is not that it isn't possible, but that it wasn't managed well, either by the business or the individual. We have to protect our own boundaries. If they are being overstepped we have to stop, think about it, and address it.

SHARING YOUR BOUNDARIES

If no one other than you knows your boundaries, it will be ex- tremely difficult to live by them. Don't be afraid to share and discuss your expectations. This might mean speaking to your family and friends as well as your manager or supervisor, and your colleagues and co-workers. In order for people to understand and accommodate a different way of working, they need to understand what you want to do and why. When I say why, it doesn't have to be in detail, nor does it have to be all about family. In fact, you have as much right, legally, to request part-time working to spend all day sitting in your underpants watching *The Simpsons* and have it seriously considered by your employer, as to request it in order to look after your children or elderly parents.

I realized, once, that I felt worse telling someone that I had to leave the office in order to get to a tennis match than I did when it was because I had to collect the children. But I shouldn't feel like that. It's not only people with kids who should get to have a life outside work.

> THE REASON WHY YOU WANT TO LEAVE WORK AND HAVE TIME TO DO THINGS OUTSIDE YOUR ROLE IS NOBODY'S BUSINESS BUT YOUR OWN.

If you want to make a change to your ways of working or working patterns, you can explain the high-level reasons, for example wanting to rebalance your life, achieve Work–Life Symbiosis, have more time to focus on other things that are important to you in addition to work. You should not feel that you have to go into every detail of what you want to do and why, particularly not in order to justify it.

Having said that, if you and your employer are trying to figure out new ways of working in order for you to meet the needs and responsibilities you have outside the workplace, it may be practical and appropriate to discuss the details. But make sure you do this as part of a proactive problem-solving discussion, rather than because you feel like you need to make excuses for why you want to start doing things differently.

Consider and capture who the people are that you will need to have discussions with in order to make changes that enable you to live by your boundaries:

TO MAKE MY BOUNDARIES WORK I WILL NEED TO SPEAK TO:

....

....

....

....

....

....

....

....

....

....

....

HAVING TOUGH CONVERSATIONS

Some organizations do not have a progressive culture around people managing their own boundaries, and neither do all managers, leaders or colleagues. The likelihood is that, in order to make changes to your working patterns and practices, you will need to have some tough conversations. Being (absolutely) fabulous will help give you the credibility and confidence you need to have these discussions, and being true to yourself will ensure you know it's the right thing to do for you. There are some clear steps you can take to handle these conversations as productively and successfully as possible.

FIND THE SOLUTION

People always prefer it if you come to them with a solution rather than a problem. You have already identified the key people with whom you will need to discuss your boundaries in order to make them happen (I will refer to them as 'stakeholders'). For each of these people individually, try and put yourself in their shoes and consider what their perspective on this might be:

- What is their current context and situation as far as you know?
- What will they think of the things you want to do differently?
- How will this impact them?
- How could this be an advantage to them?
- What challenges might this cause them?
- Will they be supportive? If not, why not?

Then consider the suggestions you could make to mitigate or alleviate their concerns. Think of some different options that might meet your needs to a greater or lesser degree and that address the issues that you think your stakeholders might have. You may not be able to think of the answers, but at least if you have considered the challenges and their concerns you show that you are aware and are trying to find a constructive solution. For each of the stakeholders, complete the following table to capture their concerns and how you might propose to address them:

STAKEHOLDER	WILL THEY BE SUPPORTIVE OR NOT? YES/NO/MAYBE	WHAT WILL BE THEIR CONCERNS OR CHALLENGES?	WHAT CAN YOU SUGGEST TO MITIGATE THIS?

KNOW YOUR IMPACT

Once you are clear on the boundaries you want to share and the proposals you have to make it workable, you need to think about how you are going to put them across. There can be a big difference between what you want to communicate to someone and what he or she actually hears. So many different things can influence the way your message lands, such as your choice of words, tone, body language and manner of speaking. Things out of your control such as the mood, mindset or attitude of the person you are speaking to can also influence it.

As an HR director, I have seen so many conflict situations, disagreements, arguments, upsets and frustrations that have no foundation whatsoever and are caused purely by misunderstandings: the receiver of the message simply not understanding the message in the way it was intended. It happens incredibly easily, but can be avoided.

I fell foul of this the first time I managed someone. I was very excited about being a manager and really wanted to do a good job – to be a good boss. I had thought long and hard about the sort of manager I wanted to be, and prepared carefully for our first meeting. Unfortunately, I did not have the impact I intended at all. The following cartoon demonstrates not what was being said, but what each of us was **thinking** during the course of our initial meeting:

Fortunately we built such a strong relationship that, a while later, we were able to discuss this first meeting and reflect, with a great deal of laughter, how it had played out.

There are two key things to help ensure you have the impact that you intend:

1. **Ask for feedback.** It's impossible to know, intuitively, how you come across. You have to ask people to find out. Regularly asking for feedback will help you understand your impact on people and situations, and help you to be the person you want to be – the person you committed to being on your Lifeboard.

Feedback can help to build your confidence, but it can also sometimes be difficult to hear. That doesn't make it any less important. If you are concerned about what people might say, pick someone that you trust and speak to them first before asking a wider group. Always explain that you are asking for their help in them giving you feedback, that it's important to you for them to be honest, that you won't judge or be annoyed with them (then you need to make sure you aren't – whether you like what they say or not, it's still the way you came across to them), and that you want this information to help you grow and develop as a person. Once you feel comfortable, try the following:

- **Get a feel for your impact.** Pick five to seven people with whom you work closely, or are good friends if you are focusing outside work, and ask them to write down the first five words that spring to mind about you. If you are nervous about this, or want to focus on building your confidence, you could ask specifically for only positive words to start with. In the end though, it's important know the whole picture. Once you get this information, try to identify the themes that come out, and then consider whether this is what you want them to be. Feedback of this sort tends to be relatively consistent. Then understand why you come across this way, which could involve more detailed discussions with some of the people that gave you the feedback. Ask them for examples of why they gave those words – seek to understand not to defend or dispel. Then you can think about the behaviours and approaches you could try that mean you come across in future more often in the way that you intend.

- **Understand the message you give.** When you have a particular message to put across in a conversation or presentation, or a certain impact you want to make with an individual, ask the recipients afterwards how they experienced you. This allows you to ascertain whether you came across in the way that you wanted to and whether the message they took away was the one you intended them to. This can be done in a structured approach by specifically asking someone after a meeting, and explaining to them that you are seeking this feedback to check the way you came across. It can also be done as part of the general conversation at the time, which is a technique I would recommend. At the end of the discussion, just ask the person you are talking with to summarize back what they've heard and explain that this is to ensure that you both have the same joint understanding. This gives you the opportunity in the moment to correct any misinterpretations and is a good habit to get into.

2. **Build big relationships.** The bigger the relationships you have with people, the more leeway you have with everything you do!

> WE ALL FORGIVE THOSE WE LIKE OR LOVE MORE THAN THOSE WE ARE LESS FOND OF. IT'S HUMAN NATURE.

You don't need to be best friends with people you work with if you don't want to. But you do need to have functional and effective work relationships, and that means openness, honesty, kindness and consideration. In my experience, there is <u>always</u> a level on which you can connect with somebody. There's always something you have in common, or something they have to say that is interesting. Find the common ground and you find a connection. Find a connection and it's much easier to build the relationship. It might be about a sport you both like, about family, you may have travelled to the same places or studied similar things, you may both like gardening, have mutual friends through work, or have both recently bought a house or car. It may be that your partners have the same interests.

Whatever it is, it doesn't take long to find. Just have an open conversation, ask them about themselves and something will emerge that interests you and you can relate to. Then, take care of your relationship. You may be busy and stressed out, with too many things to do, but likely so are they – if there's an opportunity to do something to help or support them, try and find a way to do it. The stronger your relationship, the easier it is to deal with the tough days when you don't come across in the way that you intended, or when you have to have a tough conversation with them about something.

UNDERSTAND EACH OTHER'S STORY

You have already considered for each of your stakeholders what you think their current context and perspective on your situation and suggestions might be. This makes you more sensitive to their needs, and more empathetic. It allows you to prepare suggestions that you think might meet their needs. But remember,

THERE'S NO SUBSTITUTE FOR ACTUALLY ASKING THEM WHAT THEY THINK.

I remember once I had an important meeting. It was a crucial milestone in a piece of work that was a significant priority for me. I had put the meeting in the diary a long time ago and I expected my colleague to be prepared and on the ball to make some tough decisions. I had put a great deal of time and effort into preparing for it, and had left home particularly early that morning to get into the office in plenty of time to be ready.

She turned up late – half an hour late. Not only that, but she was not prepared, she did not seem focused, couldn't remember some of our previous conversations and was certainly not being decisive. I was annoyed – I felt that she had let me down and hadn't made the effort she should have made. This came across, as I wasn't very good at hiding my emotions at that point. In my first management position I was nicknamed 'poker face', sarcastically of course, because I was so poor at hiding my reactions and feelings in meetings, good or bad! Anyway, in turn she got annoyed as well, and the meeting was pretty disastrous.

It turned out that her daughter had been ill the night before. She had been up all night looking after her and had not managed to get any sleep at all. She had no sleep **at all**. She had wanted to stay off work to look after her daughter but had made other arrangements **exactly because** she knew how important this meeting was to me and did not want to let me down. She had behaved with enormous commitment to me as well as the work we were doing. In fact, she made a personal sacrifice to be there.

When she had arrived at the meeting I could see she didn't look herself, but I was so caught up in my annoyance that she was late that I didn't ask that one simple question which would have completely changed the course of both of our days "Are you ok?" I felt awful when I realized what had happened, as you can imagine.

NOW I ALWAYS ASK HOW SOMEONE IS,
EVEN IF THEY TURN
UP ON TIME AND LOOKING THEIR BEST!

I also try very hard not to make assumptions about why someone is or is not doing or saying something, or about the intentions behind it. It was Oscar Wilde who so wisely said

**When you assume, you make an 'ass'
out of 'u' and 'me'.**

A classic quote, I think you'll agree! Often things are not as they seem and it is extremely important, particularly when you are discussing something with someone that is difficult or important, to ensure that you both truly understand each other's perspectives and intentions.

BE HONEST

In my experience, honesty really is the best policy. I know that if you work in sales or are negotiating important contracts then laying it all on the line upfront may not be the most strategic or effective approach. But when it comes to individual conversations about things that are personally important to you, my approach is just to say what you really think and how you really feel. I find people appreciate that, and respond accordingly.

The first time I ever did a piece of consultancy work I wasn't really sure how much to charge. I felt that I had a good relationship with the client and I trusted her but we hadn't worked together before and didn't know each other that well. So when we talked money, I just explained. I said that it was my first piece of consultancy, I wasn't exactly sure what my daily rate should be, so I was going to tell her what I was thinking of charging and I would appreciate her being honest and telling me whether she thought I was over-selling or under-selling myself. She appreciated that I had been so straightforward rather than just trying to charge as much as I could, and she suggested my fee should actually be more than I had proposed. Honesty pays – literally!

This includes being honest about how you feel. When left unsaid, feelings can get in the way of how you respond to someone, how you perceive them or how you interpret what they say. And this goes both ways. When you're having a discussion about a difficult topic, make space both to explain how the situation makes you feel and to hear how the situation and perhaps your suggestions make the other person feel. Sometimes these feelings may need time to be digested, and even if someone reacts defensively at first, very often after time to reflect, they respond differently.

BE OPEN TO COMPROMISE

We've talked already about the need for flexibility to reasonably accommodate the needs of your organization. In any discussions about ways of working or working patterns it's important to be open to compromise. There may be elements that you haven't considered, or challenges that might be caused by your proposals that you hadn't thought of or can't resolve.

Listen openly to the thoughts of the person you are talking to. Their concerns and suggestions matter, and you may have to compromise in order to create something that works for both of you. It may turn out that between you you come up with a better solution than the one you originally suggested.

BE CLEAR ABOUT YOUR MESSAGE

When we have a lot we want to put across, particularly if it's a conversation we perceive could be difficult, it can be easy for our key message to be lost. Make sure you are crystal-clear beforehand on the two or three key points that you really want to ensure you land in your conversation. For example, it might be:

- You are very committed to your role and to the organization.
- The way you are working currently is not sustainable.
- You want to work together with your boss to find a solution that works for you and for them.

Of course, there may be lots of other information or suggestions you want to put across or discuss during the meeting, but make sure that the key points don't get lost – say them at the start and reiterate them at the end!

If you want further guidance on how to manage difficult conversations or if this is one of the things you are most concerned about, read *Difficult Conversations* by Douglas Stone, Bruce Patton and Sheila Heen (published in 1999). It is one of the most useful books I've ever read. It is extremely helpful, makes complete sense and is easy to read. The world would be a better place if everyone had read this book.

MAKING A COMMITMENT

Pull together everything we've covered in this chapter to complete your action plan below about how you will create, implement and live by your boundaries.

ACTION PLAN TO ENABLE CRYSTAL-CLEAR BOUNDARIES

MY BOUNDARIES STATEMENT IS:

WHAT IS NOT ACCEPTABLE FOR ME IS:

MY IDEAS TO MAKE THIS WORK ARE:

THE RISKS OF THIS ARE:

THE ACTIONS I CAN TAKE
TO MITIGATE THESE RISKS ARE:

THE PEOPLE I NEED TO DISCUSS THIS WITH ARE:

THE ACTIONS I WILL TAKE TO MAKE THESE CONVERSATIONS
SUCCESSFUL ARE:

CHAPTER

CHAPTER 6

WHAT TO DO NEXT

'HE-MAN' MOMENTS

How we feel about a situation can depend a great deal on whether we feel we are in a power**ful** or power**less** position. I can't emphasize enough how important it is to feel that you have choices, that you are in control, that you are empowered. He-Man may not have been your favoured superhero when you were growing up (though he was mine for a while), but he had it right when he held his sword up and said

I HAVE THE POWER

I wish I had an example of a female superhero from my childhood who was as empowered. There was of course She-Ra, Princess of Power, who I think came close, but she didn't have quite such an effective catch phrase as He-Man. For me, though, He-Man was effectively gender neutral – it was not to do with the fact that he was a man that I thought he was great, it was because he was able to transform himself into a powerful hero when he needed to. That's a cool trick for anyone, male or female.

When you feel that you have options and that you are in control of your destiny you are far better placed to cope with life's challenges and setbacks. You are also far more likely to be bold and make the choices that align your life with what's really important to you.

I don't know about you, but when it comes to negotiating I'm not very good, especially about money. It all feels very awkward and uncomfortable. I learnt a number of years ago though how important it is both to feel and act as if you have other options – have the power balance in your favour. My partner and I were in Thailand. We had been out for the evening and were heading back to our hotel. The walk wasn't far, and it was a nice evening. There were lots of tuk tuk drivers around waiting to drive tourists like us home for an extortionate fee.

I quite fancied a tuk tuk ride because it looked fun and I was tired, but I could take it or leave it really. A guy offered us a ride and gave us a price. It was absurdly expensive. I know that's how it works, they start high and you negotiate down to something reasonable but I've never been very good at that. I always feel awkward, and I also generally always really want whatever it is I am attempting to buy, which the seller can spot a mile off.

In this case we were perfectly happy to walk, and would only have seriously considered paying for a tuk tuk if it was a reasonable price. Usually when I try to negotiate I discuss, explain, ask questions. In this case I just said no thanks, it was too expensive, and walked away. While I was walking away, without even looking back, the guy carried on shouting to me, dropping his price over and over again. In the end, he was offering it at so much less than he originally did that I thought, ok, that's reasonable now, why not?

The funny thing was, I hadn't said anything at all, I had just shown very clearly by physically walking away, that I really wasn't interested at that price. I had all the power from a negotiating perspective. I would genuinely rather have walked home than pay more than I felt was a fair price.

In the end we tipped him generously because his ride was fun and he was nice, so he probably ended up with the amount of money in his pocket he'd originally hoped for.

But that is not the point.

That is the position we need to be in in life. In all the years I've worked, I have always felt that I would genuinely rather leave an organization and work somewhere else than accept a working situation that compromised the rest of my life. When you feel like that, you are just like He-Man – you have the power. If the situation is not acceptable to you as it is, you need to feel empowered to take it into your own hands, and do something about it. You have a choice.

Fortunately I have never felt unhappy with my working situation, or the expectation of the organizations I have worked in. But I know other people in the same organizations who have. So why is that? It's not luck, it's because I fiercely protect my boundaries. I am able to do this because I have always felt that I have a choice; that the ball is in my court. As a result I have never felt scared to push back in order to maintain a working arrangement I am happy with and that works for my whole life.

I have been aware that there is risk attached to that – my line manager or colleagues may not like it. But it's very important to me, so I take that risk knowing that the worst-case scenario isn't all that bad actually. In fact, it's my plan B.

Let's consider that for a moment. What is the worst-case scenario? You have the working pattern you are happy with because you've fiercely protected your boundaries, but the organization you're in or the people you work for make it clear that this way of working is not acceptable to them.

OK, fine, I'll go and work somewhere it is acceptable. That's my plan B.

But no one has ever done that. Despite the fact that I have often worked fewer hours than those around me, who regularly worked into the evening, no one has ever told me I needed to work more. So I wonder how many people out there work longer hours and at weekends because they think it would not be acceptable to do fewer hours, when actually, it would be perfectly fine. They are scared of something that may never happen.

It's easy to feel, or be made to feel, like you 'have a good deal' in a particular job or company – that it will be harder elsewhere. But the truth is there really are loads of different types of organizations, businesses, opportunities and ways of working out there to be discovered. If the situation you're in now doesn't work for you, find one that does.

I have heard people say they are unhappy with their current situation but that there are some good things about it. As a result, they dare not take the risk of going elsewhere because somewhere new might be worse. But that doesn't change the fact that they are unhappy now. Embrace the idea that 'a change is as good as a rest' and go for it.

Even if a new job or organization isn't better, it will still be refreshing, exciting and invigorating to go somewhere new, meet new people and take on new challenges. If after you've settled in you genuinely feel that it wasn't the right move, which in my experience is unlikely, you can make another change. The fact is you will have taken action – taken your fate into your own hands and done something about the fact that you were unhappy. Even if it isn't quite right, I bet it will turn out to be a step in the right direction to finding what is the right move for you.

So it's important to have a plan B. If you have some of the difficult conversations we talked about in chapter 5, you need to feel that it's ok if the answer you get in response is "no", because you have a plan B that is perfectly sufficient. This means you hold all the cards – it means

YOUR HAPPINESS IS NOT SUBJECT TO SOMEONE ELSE'S DECISION.

Your plan B could be any number of different things ranging from finding another job either in the same company or in a different one, setting up your own business, doing contract work. Or it could be as simple as accepting the current situation and finding the positives in it, which might be the people around you that you can learn from, the opportunities it might lead to, the money you are earning, the easy journey to work.

Whatever it is, find your way to feel empowered.

So the answer to the question I mentioned in the Introduction, when people ask me how I am able to regularly work acceptable hours and not often at weekends, is simple. It's because I don't want to. So I don't. I manage my workload to allow this and I take the risk that others may not like it. If they ever don't, I'll cross that bridge when I come to it.

So far so good.

IT'S ALL CONNECTED

You've worked through the four elements of the Work–Life Symbiosis model and so you now have the following:

- A Lifeboard showing clearly what is most important to you in life so that you can **be true to yourself.**
- A picture of what enables you to be totally on form, and an understanding of what is or is not in your control; a better understanding of your circadian rhythm, how to maintain concentration, be

more active, have a positive mindset, be more mindful and get enough sleep. These all allow you to **be (absolutely) fabulous.**

- A view of what is urgent and what is important, and some actions as a result of this. As well as a plan about how to say "no" more, how to use your commuting time, what to stop doing, how to be effective personally, and how to take tough priority calls. You also have a plan about managing the right stakeholders. This enables you **to ruthlessly prioritize.**

- A boundaries statement and a clear understanding of what is not acceptable to you. As well as an understanding of how to make this work, how to mitigate the risks and how to manage the tough conversations that might be needed. This enables to you to have **crystal-clear boundaries.**

As well as each of these four elements being critical on their own, the way in which they interact with and support each other is important to remember – it's the interaction that gives you the symbiosis.

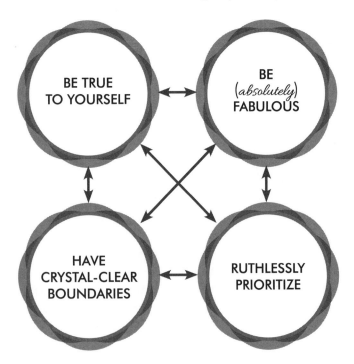

Being true to yourself gives you direction about what to align your priority choices behind and informs your boundaries. It also allows you to know what you want to be (absolutely) fabulous at. Being clear about your life priorities gives you the confidence to feel empowered because you know what matters the most and therefore if someone or something is not enabling this, you know it's time to make a different choice.

Being (absolutely) fabulous gives you the credibility and voice for the difficult conversations needed to manage your boundaries, and increases your chances of being given the right opportunities. It gives you the energy and positivity to be true to yourself, and let's face it life is more fun when we are being our best self.

Ruthlessly prioritizing makes managing your boundaries easier and enables you to focus on the important things, like being true to yourself. It also enables you to be (absolutely) fabulous.

Having crystal-clear boundaries helps you to be (absolutely) fabulous because you are deriving energy from all areas of your life. It enables you to be true to yourself and forces you to prioritize ruthlessly.

LIFE IS UNPREDICTABLE

If someone asked you ten years ago, even five years ago, what your life would be like now I am pretty confident you would not have guessed half of it. That's what makes life so much fun – we don't know how things will pan out. You need to embrace this and re-member that choices you make don't have to be 'forever' choices, they can be what's right for you now. As you go through life, your priorities will inevitably change and evolve, and so too should the choices you make. I think keeping this in mind can help to take away the pressure of making changes in your life – you don't have to feel that they are forever, they are the right thing for now.

My core values are the same as they were five years ago, but my Lifeboard is not and so my choices are not either.

This unpredictable, and often unexpected, nature of life was brought home to me once when I was sitting in a hotel bar waiting to meet my team to treat them to afternoon tea. I couldn't help but overhear the conversation the two women on the table next to me were having. One of them was having treatment for cancer. She had also won the lottery. Talk about two extremes.

I have heard stories of couples who have lifetime ambitions that they plan to fulfil in their retirement but sadly soon after they retire one of them passes away and they never get the chance to live those dreams. If only they'd done it sooner.

YOU NEVER KNOW WHAT WILL HAPPEN IN LIFE, SO DON'T WAIT - DO IT NOW!

Be clear on the good things in your life and in your job – it's important not to overlook those. But if those good things are not good enough, make a change. Put your plan B into action.

MAKING A COMMITMENT

So, you've read this book, or maybe you've just cut straight to the final chapter, but either way you're reading this now and I'm interpreting that as an intention to make some changes in your life. Do it. As I said in chapter 1, my message to you is this:

TAKE CONTROL - IT'S YOUR LIFE.
KNOW WHAT'S REALLY IMPORTANT.
MAKE CHOICES AND ACCEPT THE CONSEQUENCES.
REMEMBER THAT THE ONLY PERSON THAT

CAN MAKE A CHANGE Is YOU.
AND WHATEVER YOU DO, DON'T HAVE REGRETs.

You've got all the tools and action plans now, but having them on paper will not make any difference. You have to act on them. What are you going to do differently, starting tomorrow? Write it down and be committed.

I WANT WORK–LIFE SYMBIosIs, SO TOMORROW I AM GoING To:

....

....

....

....

....

....

....

....

....

....

....

And remember what Gandhi said:

**Happiness is not something ready made.
It comes from your own actions.**

FURTHER READING

These are the books have that have been the most influential in shaping my thinking:

Difficult Conversations by Douglas Stone, Bruce Patton and Sheila Heen. Penguin Books, 1999.

The 7 Habits of Highly Effective People by Stephen R. Covey. Free Press, 1989.

Lean In: Women, Work and the Will to Lead by Sheryl Sandberg. W H Allen, 2013.

Free! Love your work, love your life by Chris Barez-Brown. Penguin Books, 2014.

ABOUT THE AUTHOR

Claire Fox is an experienced Human Resources Director who has worked in the field for more than 15 years in global and local roles. She spent a significant period of time in a professional multinational FMCG, having started her career in an entrepreneurial, fast-growth start-up. She now works as a Global Human Resources Director for Save the Children International.

Claire is a Fellow of the Chartered Institute of Personnel and Development (FCIPD) and has a Masters degree in Management.

She is also a qualified fitness instructor and competed for the England senior team and Great Britain junior team as a white water slalom canoeist for a number of years. Claire captained the Great Britain junior team to the World Championships and currently captains a tennis team.

She has two children, aged three and four, and has worked part-time for the last three years so that she can enjoy plenty of time with them.

BEYOND
THE WRITTEN WORD

Authors who speak to you face to face.

Discover LID Speakers, a service that enables businesses to have direct and interactive contact with the best ideas brought to their own sector by the most outstanding creators of business thinking.

- A network specialising in business speakers, making it easy to find the most suitable candidates.

- A website with full details and videos, so you know exactly who you're hiring.

- A forum packed with ideas and suggestions about the most interesting and cutting-edge issues.

- A place where you can make direct contact with the best in international speakers.

- The only speakers' bureau backed up by the expertise of an established business book publisher.

LID speakers
.com
Sure value.

22

years

building on our success

- 1993 Madrid
- 2007 Barcelona
- 2008 Mexico DF & Monterrey
- 2010 London
- 2011 New York & Buenos Aires
- 2012 Bogota
- 2014 Shanghai & San Francisco